RELATIONSHIPS THAT WORK

Teaching is an extremely gratifying profession, but it can also be draining if you don't have fulfilling relationships and the ability to avoid toxic, negative people. This unique book, written by bestselling author and psychologist Adam Sáenz and child/adolescent therapist Jeremy Dew, shows you how to increase job satisfaction and personal fulfilment by connecting with others. You'll learn about the relationships you can forge with students, colleagues, and parents to foster a healthy and life-changing learning environment, while also avoiding social and personal stress. In particular, you'll uncover how to:

♦ Build bridges to connect with students in a positive manner, making a difference in their lives.

♦ Interact with colleagues and parents in productive ways.

♦ Examine and evaluate your professional relationships.

♦ Build fences to protect yourself from harm or frustration and remain relationally engaged.

♦ Manage your emotions effectively, and learn how to express and direct them appropriately in the classroom.

Throughout each chapter, you'll find strategies, reflection questions, and assessment tools to help you apply the book's concepts. *Relationships That Work* is an essential read for teachers at all grade levels who want not only to educate but also to guide, nurture, encourage, and form deep, long-lasting bonds.

Adam Sáenz is Founder and Clinical Director of the Oakwood Collaborative, a counseling and assessment center in Bryan, Texas.

Jeremy Dew is a licensed professional counselor who works with children and adolescents.

RELATIONSHIPS THAT WORK

Four Ways to Connect (and Set Boundaries) with Colleagues, Students, and Parents

Adam Sáenz and Jeremy Dew

Routledge
Taylor & Francis Group

NEW YORK AND LONDON

First published 2016
by Routledge
711 Third Avenue, New York, NY 10017

and by Routledge
2 Park Square, Milton Park, Abingdon, Oxon, OX14 4RN

Routledge is an imprint of the Taylor & Francis Group, an informa business

Library of Congress Cataloging-in-Publication Data
Saenz, Adam.
    Relationships that work : four ways to connect (and set boundaries)
with colleagues, students, and parents / by Adam Saenz and Jeremy
Dew. — 1 [edition].
        pages cm
    1. Teachers—Professional relationships.   2. Interaction analysis
in education.   I. Title.
    LB1775.S25 2015
    371.102'3—dc23
    2015000223

ISBN: 978-1-138-84302-8 (hbk)
ISBN: 978-1-138-84303-5 (pbk)
ISBN: 978-1-315-73118-6 (ebk)

Typeset in Palatino
by Apex CoVantage, LLC

From Adam:

For my great-grandfather, José de la Luz Sáenz:
A rare intellect, a passionate educator and a valiant
civil rights activist.

> *"They discovered what they expected to find."*
> From *The World War I Diary of José de la*
> *Luz Sáenz* (Texas A&M University Press, p. 395)

From Jeremy:

This book is for Paul Steinke, who models calling as
if he's actually called to model calling.

Contents

About the Authors

Dr. Adam Sáenz earned his Ph.D. in School Psychology from Texas A&M University. He completed his predoctoral clinical training under a fellowship appointment to Harvard Medical School, and he has a postdoctorate in clinical psychology from the Alpert Medical School of Brown University. Dr. Sáenz also earned a Doctorate of Ministry in Pastoral Counseling from Graduate Theological Foundation with residency at Christ Church College of the University of Oxford.

Dr. Sáenz is a featured blogger for the Huffington Post Education Page, and he currently serves as the clinical director of the Oakwood Collaborative, the counseling and assessment clinic he founded in 2003.

Jeremy Dew is a licensed professional counselor who has worked with children and adolescents informally in various contexts since 2001. Upon completing his graduate degree in counseling at The Seattle School, he served as an Assistant Instructor there from 2010–13. He also worked as a mental health therapist at Atlantic Street Center in Seattle from 2009–12, and has conducted professional workshops with educators for the last few years regarding self-care and its impact on their work in the classroom.

Acknowledgments

From Adam:

Thank you, Lauren Davis for your encouragement and direction as the manuscript evolved. You and the team at Routledge are absolutely top notch.

Thank you, colleagues at the Oakwood Collaborative: Katie Martin Kainer, Jackie Womack, James and Kellie Deegear, Erin Sandoval, and Thad Norvell. Thank you, Jeremy Dew, for your commitment to understand children and for the outstanding clinical work you bring to our group.

I am grateful to the many educators I've had the privilege to encounter over the course of my travels. I'm especially grateful to two in particular—administrators who gave me back-stage passes into their lives and onto their campuses: Don Beatty and Kris Mitzner.

Thank you to the Katy Independent School District for your commitment to prioritizing the relational aspects of education, and to Chris Porter for inviting me back to be a part of the district's First Year Teacher staff development and support.

Thank you, Kim, Alisa, Mya, Isaiah, and Andrew. Each of you inspires me to excel in my capacities to reflect, direct, connect and protect.

From Jeremy:

I am thankful for two of my uniquely gifted teachers, Mrs. Lynn Yarbrough in sixth grade and Sra. Mary Ann Biesiada in high school, who both offered a classroom every day that told me I was loved, but that I couldn't make the rules. I am certain that you are both key reasons why I care so deeply about my work with teachers in bringing your best selves to work.

For my fellow learners at The Seattle School: To the faculty and staff, namely Paul Steinke, Steve Call, Dan Allender, and Roy Barsness, Jon DeWaal, as well as Trapper Lukaart and Ralph Fragale—you have deeply impacted me in my sense of calling—in exploring the peaks and valleys of my life with immense kindness and curiosity, and in your commitment to me and to my growth as a therapist and a brother.

To my brothers over the last seven years—Lucas Abernathy, Chris Roberts, Troy Tiberi, and Campbell White—I am thankful most for your friendship as fellow therapists and colleagues who walk alongside me in my work and life beyond this work.

Mom and Dad, you guys have had unending energy and encouragement for my passions and pursuits, and that has had a huge impact on my resolve to pursue this work.

Brady and Elliott—you have offered me so much kindness in our year of transition to my new place of work here. I am thankful for the ways that you call me to forgiveness and humility as my sons, and for your unending desire to play and your invitation to play.

And to Jen, I am so grateful for where our professional lives continue to integrate more and more. Your voice is equally present in this book as mine is, as you have given me so much perspective on your gifts and struggles as an educator. Thank you, most of all, for the ways that you invite me to live, and for your continued pursuit of me, as well as your continued receiving from me.

Thank you, Adam, for the opportunity to join you in this venture. Your trust and your kindness as a business partner have been humbling from the start, and I look forward to the years ahead of where this community we are making will take us as a team.

"I know who I am. I am Lou Sáenz. It's my job to make your life hell. I'll never learn."

Adam Louis Sáenz, to the arresting police officer

"We never know which lives we influence, or how, or why."

Stephen King, 11/22/63

Introduction
A Tale of Two Campuses

By the time we arrived to the police station, the handcuffs had worn blisters on the back of my wrists. Mario saw them.

"Quedate con los manos asi" ("Put your hands like this"), Mario instructed me. Seated in his chair, he turned his upper torso and showed me his hands behind his back, with his fingers clasped together, as if he were praying. His handcuffs seemed to fall relaxed, between the palms of his hands. I had been fighting mine, thinking that if I pulled hard enough, I would somehow stretch them to relieve the pressure. The drugs in my system clearly were clouding my thinking. I followed his instruction and clasped my hands together. Instant relief.

We were caught red-handed with what I estimated to be about four ounces of marijuana. The officers showed up seemingly out of nowhere—it must have been an anonymous tip—and cornered Mario and me in the abandoned house. Norman, who was holding another half-pound, jumped out a window and fled on foot to evade arrest. There were witnesses. I had always been the kind of kid that could talk his way out of a paper bag, but I doubted very seriously that I was going to talk my way out of this one: Where did the drugs come from? What was I doing in an abandoned house? If we weren't doing anything wrong, why did Norman run?

I was worried. This was my first time to be arrested, my first time to be hauled to jail in the back seat of a police car, and my first time to be fingerprinted. Acting out at school was nothing new to me—office referrals, discipline reports, paddlings, suspensions. I was a veteran by those standards. But this? An arrest off school property? Somehow I knew this was a defining moment for me. I had crossed a boundary. I had cast my lot with *that* group of kids. I thought back to the conversation I overheard several weeks before between two teachers about a student who had been arrested.

"Well, what do you expect from a kid like *that*?" one teacher asked, apparently not trying too hard to contain her condescension.

The other teacher chuckled.

"You know, I think it's their job to make our lives hell," she responded. "You'd think their parents would give a damn. I just don't get it."

Given all this, I couldn't figure out why Mario seemed so calm. Then I realized: Mario had been in this situation before. Mario was four years older than me. This wasn't his first arrest or car ride or fingerprinting. He was a veteran by these standards. He knew the drill. He knew we probably would be read the riot act. He knew we probably would not be detained if our parents were located. He knew that the worst-case scenario probably would be that we'd be looking at six months' probation and maybe some community service. Piece of cake.

An angry voice interrupted my thoughts.

"We finally found your mom," the officer barked at me. The frustration in his voice seemed to imply that if my mother cared the slightest bit about her kids, he wouldn't have had to sacrifice life and limb to find her between 4:15 and 7:00 p.m. on a Tuesday evening. "She said she's on her way. But I guarantee you, if she's not here in the next twenty minutes, I'm just gonna lock you up for the night, and we can work this out with the judge tomorrow."

Eighteen minutes later, my mother arrived. I'll never forget the first words out of her mouth when she saw me.

"What are you doing here?" she demanded, her tone even angrier than the officers had been.

Here's why the question made such an impression on me. It wasn't a question of action. *What am I doing here? Well, I'm just sitting here with these handcuffs digging into my wrists, wondering what the next forty-eight hours of my life are going to look like.*

No, it wasn't a question of action. It was a question of identity, and I knew it. I remember thinking that she could not have asked me a more stupid question.

My identity? I know who I am. I am Adam Louis Sáenz. I have a miserable family life. I have no father. I have a mother who is physically present, but engages emotionally only when she wants to express anger, frustration, and bitterness. I hate school. More precisely, I hate the teachers at my school. The only escape I have from these feelings of sadness, anger, and fear are the thirty-minute reprieves I get on the back end of the fattest joint I can possibly roll. The only intimacy and community I experience is with the comparably trouble-ridden peers who hit that joint with me for exactly the same reasons I do. The only sense of empathy I know—the only way I know someone else knows how I feel—is through my headphones, through music.

All this, and the first words out of my mother's mouth are "What are you doing here?"

Are you kidding me? Isn't the more appropriate question, given who I am, "Where else would I be?"

What I suspected Mario knew was, in fact, right. We were read the riot act, we exchanged a series of threats and promises, but we were not detained. I was discharged from the harsh realities of detention back to the harsh realities of my relationally isolated life.

My mother and I didn't speak on the way home. We pulled into the driveway at 10:30 p.m. I followed my mother into the front door, walked straight into the kitchen, and devoured our last two cans of potted meat. I finally fell asleep about 2:15 a.m.

———————

Somewhere across town, Mr. Travis was sleeping. Probably. I don't know for sure, and for the life of me, I wish I could have been a fly on the wall in that teacher's home for just that one evening. How had *his* evening gone? For that matter, how had his *life* gone? How did he end up in the field of education? Was he teaching because he valued children, or was he just needing a paycheck until something better came along? Was he living a relationally engaged, vibrant life, or was he, like me, interpersonally isolated and miserable?

Why did we hate each other?

7:00 a.m. comes early the morning after one is arrested. My mom opened my bedroom door.

"You're late. Hurry up and get ready for school."

I dragged myself out of bed, dressed, and had a bowl of cereal before walking out the door. No other words were spoken at home that morning.

As I arrived on campus, I realized that word of my arrest had made the rounds. I saw my friend J.J. He had been something of a partner in crime with me ever since I met him at the beginning of summer before the second grade. We were in the same homeroom that year, and just after the start of second grade, he invited me to tag a wooden fence in his neighborhood. He even provided the spray paint. I liked him from the get-go. By the third grade and on, J.J. and I were not allowed to be together in the same homeroom.

"I heard about last night," he said as I approached him. He looked away, down at the ground, and he spoke softly. He seemed somber, almost concerned for me. "I was playing guitar in the living room after school yesterday, and I heard a call go out on my dad's police scanner. Something about three youths with drugs. Then, my dad came in after dinner and told me that he had seen you down at the station." His dad was the deputy sheriff.

"Yeah," I said, nonchalantly. "It was no big deal. They let us go. They're after Norman. He's got the connection."

I was trying to minimize. Now that I was on campus, and it was clear that everyone knew, I wasn't sure that I was quite ready to have joined the ranks I seemed to have joined. But the damage was done. None of my other classmates really said anything to me that day, but the quiet looks seemed to ask all the questions: What happened to you? Perhaps more importantly, what *is happening* to you? Can I trust you?

I managed to make it to third period before it was school business as usual.

"I just wanted to let you know you made a zero on the test," Mr. Travis announced to me as the rest of the class walked in, trying to beat the tardy bell. I wasn't even in his classroom at that point in the morning. He had come across the hall and stepped into Ms. Minor's class to make his point.

"What?" I asked. I was exhausted and slumped in my chair. I wasn't sure I heard him correctly.

"The. Test." he said, emphasizing each word. "I. Gave. You. A. Zero. Because. I. Know. You. Cheated."

He smiled.

I thought back to the test I had just taken in his science class during second period. I forget the details, but we were to use a basic formula to calculate some form of plant growth. I was still waking up and too tired to write out my work, so I just did the calculation in my head, wrote down the answer, turned in my test, and spent the rest of his class with my head down on my desk.

"I didn't cheat," I said. "I did the calculations in my head and just wrote down the answer!" I was loud.

By this time, both Mr. Travis and I were aware that we had an audience. He walked a few steps closer to me.

"There's no way you could have done that math in your head and come up with the right answer," he said as he shot back a look of disdain. "Look," he continued, pointing his index finger at my face, "I know you're a cheater. Now don't be a liar, too."

Then, he crossed his arms and smiled. Again. And with that, I was done.

"You know what?" I yelled, standing up from my desk "You can fail me. You can kiss my ass, too, because I didn't cheat and I'm not lying."

The show ended. He grabbed me by the arm, and as he marched me to the principal's office, he stopped by his classroom to get the piece of wood he would use to hit me. We fumbled into the principal's office, and he slammed the door closed.

"Bend over and grab the desk," he ordered.

I complied. Slowly, though. It was my passive-aggressive attempt to retain some sense of control or power in the situation.

He then delivered three blows, each landing precisely between my hamstring and buttock, each lifting me off my feet. I kept a white-knuckle grip on the edge of the principal's desk, clamping my teeth together, hoping to avoid the expression of any form of emotion.

After the third blow, he stepped back. He tucked the piece of wood under his left arm.

"If you think that hurt," Mr. McKay, the principal, said, "you can rest assured those were love pats compared to what I'm going to do to you next time I see you back in my office."

I stood with a blank, disengaged stare, trying to detach myself from every aspect of that moment—the thoughts, the sights, the sounds. Mostly, though, the emotions. The physical pain was so severe, I couldn't sit in a chair until that afternoon. The bruising was visible across my backside for the following ten days.

As I've written this memory, I've wondered to myself if it was really *that* bad. I've wondered if this is just me—a middle-aged adult with unresolved childhood issues and an axe to grind—simply overstating facts in an attempt to portray himself as the victim of a cruel teacher. After all, given all the years that have passed since then, I will only ever know that experience through the eyes of my twelve-year-old self—my angry, relationally isolated twelve-year-old self.

After earnest introspection, though, I honestly don't believe I am overstating. Here's why: I also remember a reading teacher on that campus once commenting to the class about the t-shirt I was wearing with the logo of my favorite rock band: "Whoever listens to music like that must eat out of a garbage can." And then there was the football coach on that campus who made a habit of delivering profanity-ridden tirades to my teammates and me about how he could never have a winning season, let alone win a game with us—the rejects—he was given to coach.

As I write those memories, I must stop again: *Wait, Adam. Was it really that bad? Now it's not just Mr. Travis, but the entire faculty?*

It was not the entire faculty, no. There was Ms. Millsap—always kind, respectful, and firm. Surely there were a couple of others like her.

But as I look back and reconstruct my experience on that campus, clearly, there were enough data points to reveal a pattern. The data portrayed a professional culture that seemed to communicate the following:

> *We are not a teaching force; we are a policing force. Our primary function is to identify and extinguish all inappropriate student behavior by whatever means necessary, including shame, coercion, and power-play. Since it is us, the faculty, versus them, the students and their families, we must circle the wagons of our minds and hearts to protect ourselves from them and keep them out. They are dangerous. They are not to be trusted. We confess: this culture is soul-crushing for everyone involved. This culture was not our dream when we entered the field of education. We hoped for so much more. Yet, here we are. Stuck. And since we have resigned ourselves to being stuck, we also have given ourselves permission to engage in demonstrable commiseration, which fuels our cynicism, which allows us to distance ourselves emotionally from our students and their families, which allows us to police more effectively.*

I also know I'm not overstating my experience in that district because I know toxic-culture campuses (and districts) exist today. I've worked in them. In August 2012, I was invited to give the keynote address at a back-to-school convocation in a small Texas town. I love doing convocations—the excitement, the anticipation, the energy. It's like the ultimate sports pep-rally, but for the faculty, and as far as I'm concerned, they're the ones who deserve it. As I entered the high school auditorium in this particular district, though, I was greeted by a palpable tension: there were very few smiles and even less eye contact exchanged. I finally found the district superintendent (no one acknowledged my presence or received me as I entered, so I sought him out on my own), and I introduced myself.

"Hello, sir," I greeted him. "My name is Dr. Adam Sáenz. I will be the convocation speaker today. I'm honored to be here."

He nodded his head and gave me a stiff, firm handshake. He looked concerned.

"Glad you could be here," he said. "I will address the faculty briefly before I introduce you."

I took my seat on the front row, and after a few opening remarks by other district staff, the superintendent took the podium. These were his actual words:

> Good morning. I'm going to be honest. I know most of you don't want to be here, and I know most of you are going to try to leave early. That's why I'm making you sign in before and after this event. We will be standing in the back to make sure that none of you try to walk out early. And now, please welcome our guest speaker, Dr. Adam Sáenz.

Yes, actual words. How could I forget them? *This* was what the faculty had to look forward to as they left the down-time of summer and entered yet another nine-month exercise in frustration, anger, fear and hopelessness. As I took the stage, I wondered what I could possibly impart to this faculty that would make any difference in the context of their relational culture. I felt an overwhelming sadness.

Fortunately for those of us who work in education, for those of us who have children that attend public schools, such districts and campuses are not the norm—in Texas or across the country. Fortunately for me, I've experienced something other.

———————

Child Protective Services was never involved with my family, but my mother could read the writing on the wall. As a sixth-grader, I was already becoming the wrong crowd; I had an older brother who was at risk for dropping out of high school. At the end of that school year, my mother started searching for options. Phone calls were made ("*It doesn't look good for him . . . would you consider? . . . you could send him back down on holidays"*). Then, legal documents were signed (*"hereby award temporary conservatorship . . . assess his subsequent adjustment . . . reassess if problems arise"*).

And just like that, I was living with family friends in Katy, Texas. Anyone familiar with Houston knows that Katy is now part of Houston's urban sprawl (the district recently opened its eighth high school and continues to grow, both in population and in cultural diversity). In the early 1980s, though, Katy was different. Much different. Back then, Katy was a tiny rice-farming town out in the sticks with one elementary, one junior high, and one high school. Having grown up in the 95 percent Hispanic population of the Rio Grande Valley of south Texas, I felt very out-of-place. That summer felt particularly brief, and before I knew it, I was headed out the door for my first day of school.

What a different school experience.

My principal at Katy Junior High—Mr. Roosevelt Alexander—knew about my past when I arrived to Katy (my guardian had given him a brief history about how I landed in Katy). Looking back, I'm guessing that Mr. Alexander knew that a kid like me probably had repeated negative interactions with authority figures, and as a result, probably had issues with people in positions like his. I did. On the second day of school, I saw him standing on the steps by the school's front door, and I avoided eye contact as I approached, not wanting to have anything to do with him. I looked up, and he was suddenly standing directly in front of me.

"What do you want with me?" I thought. *"I haven't been here long enough to offend anyone, and my eyes haven't been bloodshot in over four months."*

"Welcome to Katy, son," he said, extending out his right hand. "My name is Mr. Alexander. I am your principal. I'm glad you're here." He smiled, and then he patted me on the back, and then he walked away. All this, seemingly out of nowhere. I was dumbfounded. *Was this a plot? Was he setting me up?* No. For the first time in my life, as I interacted with Mr. Alexander over the course of that year, I came to know what love-based leadership really looked like.

My counselor at Katy Junior High—Mr. Roger Beck—also knew I was facing a difficult transition. Mr. Beck knew I was different from the other kids at Katy Junior High, and it wasn't just the AC/DC t-shirts I wore. Early on, he would check in with me—he was so non-threatening about it, it was weird to me—just to make sure I was doing okay.

"You've got quite a few AC/DC shirts," he once observed with a smile. "I haven't listened to them before. If you ever happen to think about it, do you think I might borrow one of their tapes from you?" His question surprised me, and I thought he was joking, so I laughed it off. The next day, though, as I was preparing to leave the house for school, I remembered, and I put *Highway to Hell* in my Trapper Keeper. I found him just before lunch.

"Here you go," I said, producing the cassette. Now it was his turn to be surprised.

"Come by my office after lunch. We'll have a listen."

I'll never forget the moment after lunch when he cued the tape in his office. Side one, song one. He pushed play. Enter a screaming Bon Scott:

> *Livin' easy, lovin' free. Season ticket on a one-way ride. Askin' nothing', leave me be. Takin' everythin' in stride. Don't need rhythm, don't need rhyme. Ain't nothin' that I'd rather do. Goin' down, party time. My friends are gonna be there too.*

By the time we got to the chorus, I thought surely I had crossed a boundary. I expected him to immediately push the stop button and lecture me about appropriate language, and aggression, and all manner of evil, including drugs, sex, and rock-and-roll. But he didn't. Instead, he listened. *To the whole freaking song!* This clearly was not his style of music, not his vibe, not his personality or reality. But he listened. He used it as a connecting point. Mr. Beck knew that from that moment on, he and I had music. He had his music, and I had my music, and good Lord, were they different. But together, we had music. For the first time in my life, I experienced someone pursuing me, someone expressing interest in me simply because they wanted to get to know me.

My track coach at Katy Junior High—Coach Obra Thompkins—knew that I was the kind of kid who, without better options, would find trouble after school somewhere off campus. Coach Thompkins approached me one afternoon while I was running on the track. Running had become this weird thing for me—running oval after oval on a track, uninterrupted, just me and my music. It was hypnotic. It was like therapy for me. As I rounded the track, Coach Thompkins held up his hand to stop me by the field house. I removed my headphones and stood looking at him, quiet, not knowing what this was about.

"I sure love the way you run, young man," he said. "You've got a great, open stride, and you look like you've got a lot of potential as a middle-distance runner. My name is Coach Thompkins, I'd be honored to work with you this coming track season." For the first time in my life, I experienced encouragement and support, someone overtly saying, "I believe in you."

By the time I left Katy Junior High and transitioned to Katy High School, I was a much more focused student. My grades had improved, and I had qualified for the Junior Olympic national cross-country meet. But much more importantly, I was a more settled human being. I was no longer operating primarily out of fear and anger as base emotions. I was more willing and able to surrender my need to control and allow the adults on campus to lead me. I was learning to give and receive love. I was learning to give and receive trust.

As I transitioned to Katy High School, the growth and healing continued. The librarian, Mrs. Betty Schmaltz, always welcomed me, always seemed genuinely happy that I chose to enter that quiet, ordered, predictable and safe sanctuary. ("I know I'll find you in the 100s," she would say, referencing my curiosity for psychology and philosophy.) My biology teacher, Mr. Ray Wolman, taught me that life is an ordered system of interdependent systems, with each system both needing and serving the other; when a system fails or disconnects from the other systems, life fails. His wife, Mrs. Jamie Wolman, was my sociology teacher, and in her class I was fascinated to learn that society is a form of collective life, also an ordered system of interdependent systems, an idea that would underpin my understanding of human behavior as a practicing psychologist many years later. And, as I recount in *The Power of a Teacher*, Mrs. JoElla Exley and Mrs. Polly McRoberts were the two English teachers that spoke—through writing—a profound truth that would guide me out of my darkest hours the year after I graduated from Katy High School.

On May 16 2014, Katy I.S.D. hosted a banquet to honor their Volunteers In Public Schools (VIPS) participants. I was honored to be invited to deliver the keynote address, almost thirty years after having graduated from Katy High School. As over a thousand volunteers and faculty packed the Merrell Center to reflect back on the school year, I took the stage.

"Hillary Rodham Clinton once said that it takes a village to raise a child," I began. "In the early 1980s, Katy, Texas was the village, and Adam Louis Sáenz was the child."

I didn't know beforehand, but several of my former teachers were in the audience that morning. As I was signing books in the front lobby of the Merrell Center following the event, I felt a hand on my shoulder. I turned and immediately recognized—over thirty years later—Coach Thompkins, still a large, imposing man. I instinctively jumped from my seat, smiled, and wrapped my arms around him. Neither of us spoke. There, in front of all the other educators and volunteers, we were two grown men, embracing each other, weeping in each other's arms, utterly caught in that moment.

Finally, I collected myself long enough to whisper, "Thank you . . . thank you . . . thank you."

"No," he whispered back. "Thank *you*."

I was confused. Thank me for what? He—and many others like him—were the ones who had given (and continue to give) so tirelessly to make an impact in kids' lives, day after day, week after week, semester after semester, year after year. I was merely the recipient.

As we pulled back from each other, the look in his eyes answered my question. I realized in that moment that my life, well-lived, was the greatest and most sincere act of gratitude I could offer him. That moment afforded him—a lifetime educator—one of those seemingly ever-evasive opportunities to actually taste the fruit of his labor. In me, he was met with undeniable evidence that he had not invested his life in vain, without reason, or without purpose. I am a measure—four simple beats—in Coach Thompkins' opus. And Mr. Alexander's. And Mr. Beck's. And Mrs. Schmaltz's. And Mr. Wolman's. And Mrs. Wolman's. And Mrs. Exley's and Mrs. McRoberts'.

They were, and are, men and women of exceptional mental and emotional capacity. Thirty years ago, other futures were available to them; they could have stepped into professional trajectories that involved stock options and company cars and ended in retirements that involved top-tier social and economic clout. They could have done and they could have been anything. Fortunately for me, and literally thousands of others like me, that's not what they were after. That's not what mattered to them in their heart of hearts. Because not only were they mentally and emotionally capable, but much more importantly, they were also wise—wise enough to know that life's greatest reward, life's richest treasure, is to be connected to another human being. So, instead of stepping into those alternate futures, they stepped into schools.

What I am doing here is not an attempt to idealize Katy I.S.D. Not every educator in that district was effective. Mike, for example, had absolutely no business teaching. Or being around kids, for that matter. He was essentially an internally miserable person who seemed intent on externalizing his misery. I'm calling him by his first name because if he's alive and discovers I called him out, he'll probably sue me. (Same thing with Mr. Travis—not his real name.) I'm sure there were and are others of his ilk in the district. The point I am making is that just as there was a culture in the district I had attended previously, there was a culture in Katy. In Katy, though, the culture was life-giving.

I wrote my first book, *The Power of a Teacher*, with two goals in mind. First, as a former student, I wanted to encourage educators. I wanted to remind readers that my life is proof that what educators do matters, proof that the educator's investment in today's students quite literally changes the future. Second, as a licensed psychologist, I wanted to equip educators. Given this high calling, self-care is critical for an educator intent on a lifetime in the vocation. I wanted to offer a practical assessment tool to measure their wellbeing, and then provide practical tools and strategies to increase wellbeing in their physical, emotional, financial, spiritual, and occupational lives.

Two years have passed since I published *The Power of a Teacher*. I have been both thrilled and humbled at the reception my story and the book have received. As I have delivered keynote addresses and presented professional development in school districts and at conferences across the country, I have been met with the same question: What did your teachers do, exactly, to connect with you, and what can I do in my classroom, specifically, to connect with my students?

The question underscores the fact that most educators already understand the importance of relationships. The question is "How?" *How do I connect with a student who looks different than me, who sounds different than me, whose values differ from mine, who faces different challenges than I faced, whose generation is different from mine?* And going a step further, how do I connect with colleagues when I feel so overwhelmed by the top-down demands that are placed on me and by the systemic stressors over which I know I have absolutely no control? And how do I connect with parents who seem to communicate that they have no interest in being bothered by me with any feedback—even good—regarding their child?

These are good, fair questions, and I think if we're honest with ourselves, we will find that the answers will give us pause. Initiating and sustaining healthy relationships in any setting—education or otherwise—requires of us deep and precious resources: our time, our energy, our attention. Do we really want to go there?

I hope you do. Here's why: that kid in your classroom? The one who is not responding favorably to your absolute-best academic and behavioral interventions (and driving you absolutely mad in the process)? The one who makes you sit out in the parking lot some mornings, not wanting to leave your car, wondering whether you should go back to school or get your real estate license? Yes, that one. That kid is me. That kid needs the investment I needed. But it's not just him—the kid who is outwardly struggling, obviously having a difficult time—that needs the investment. There is also the kid that is inwardly struggling, living the proverbial life of quiet desperation. She also needs the investment. As does every other student in your classroom. Each student in your classroom—and you—need to know that the physical and relational environment in your room is safe; the investment you make to create that space will both tire you and reward you.

One day in 1979, two young men sat handcuffed in a police station—one named Mario, one named Adam. Three years later, after continued run-ins with the law—theft, possession, evading arrest—Mario's life of petty crime ended. He was murdered while trying to buy drugs near the Mexican border. Thirty-five years later, I'm writing a book about how educators built the kinds of relationships with me that shaped my life and forged my destiny. I am grateful for the many doors that my education has opened. Let me be clear, though: education did not change my life; *educators* changed my life.

Each student in your classroom, on your campus, is both a living narrative and living a narrative. Three years from now and thirty-five years from now, each of those students will have a story to tell. It may be at a reunion. It may be at a funeral. If your name comes up as they recount their story, what will be the context? What will your students say about you? How will you want your students to remember you? Apart from the academic content that you teach, what will you want them to have learned from you?

There are variables you won't be able to control in your vocation as an educator—testing, higher-level leadership, a never-ending flow of mandates—but we believe in the midst of all that, you have power to change lives. You are shaping the future. What you do matters. We want to position you for maximum impact across the course of your vocation as an educator. We also believe that your maximum impact cannot be realized apart from healthy relationships, not only with your students, but also with their parents and your colleagues. We wrote this book to help posture you to make your optimum impact.

"Most of us end up with no more than five or six people who remember us. Teachers have thousands of people who remember them for the rest of their lives."

Andy Rooney

1

The Case for Relationships

My youngest son Andrew is a Lego fiend. Absolutely loves them. For months last year, he routinely stopped at the refrigerator door and stared at what lay pinned to it by the calendar magnet: two tickets to paradise—admission to the Lego Kidfest at the Hutchinson Convention Center in Dallas. Finally, the big day arrived, and we made the pilgrimage from College Station. The Lego Kidfest did not disappoint. It was all things Lego: robots, superheroes, car races, building contests, you name it. After a twenty-minute self-initiated orientation tour of the Convention Center floor, Andrew chose his first activity: a free build in which kids and their parents were encouraged to build a structure that would be incorporated into something of a group project. The result was spectacular—a Lego city built with thousands of Lego bricks of varying shapes, sizes and colors, built by hundreds of Lego builders of varying shapes, sizes and colors. It covered over four hundred square feet of the Convention Center floor. Structure was created from the chaos of buckets and buckets of random Lego bricks, and we had played a part. It was very satisfying.

We—humanity—are like a massive collection of Legos. Our individual pieces of human experience vary in size, shape and color, but all were designed and evolved specifically to connect one with another. When we connect with the right people the

21

When we connect with the right people the right way, we become a part of a narrative or unfolding story that gives us deeper meaning and purpose, both individually and collectively.

right way, we become a part of a narrative or unfolding story that gives us deeper meaning and purpose, both individually and collectively. That holds true universally—across cultures, across sexes, across generations, and across ideologies.

Sometimes our innate need and purpose to connect does not become obvious until we see the problematic behavior patterns and dysfunction that arise in a child that did not receive necessary physical and emotional attention throughout critical stages of early development. When a child is deprived of those ingredients critical to healthy human development, his or her relational pattern will tend to be skewed, characterized by being either inappropriately detached from or dependent on others. In more extreme cases, children with deeply impaired relational capacity are diagnosed with Reactive Attachment Disorder. They have become, in essence, Legos that have lost the basic form and shape necessary to maintain the bond.

Why are we concerned when a child lacks the capacity to initiate and sustain age-appropriate, inter-independent relationships? *It is because relationships are resources.* Many would go so far as to argue that relationships are our most important resource—in the end, far more valuable to us than money, education, or physical ability. Children who lack the capacity to appropriately access relationships as resources (and do not receive appropriate intervention), then, will grow up to be adults that are even more deeply isolated and impaired—damaging, even—as they relate with other human beings, children and adults alike.

Therein lies the root of our sense of urgency. Think about it: each student with whom we interact today represents some sphere of relational influence in the future—a future boss, a future employee, a future father, or a future mother. Maybe even a future teacher. Will their future influence be helpful or hurtful to those depending on them? As you probably already know, teachers have the power to play a critical role in the answer to that question.

Douglas Fiore, Ph.D., is a former teacher and principal who has served on faculty at the State University of West Georgia. According to Dr. Fiore,

> Teachers who create distance between themselves and their students make it exceedingly difficult for students to develop relationships with them . . . the relationships that teachers develop with students have a direct impact on the teacher's ability to teach and the [students'] ability to learn. For this reason, these relationships must be deemed vitally important.
>
> (2001)

Great Programming Skills: But Can You Interact With Other Humans?

Relational skills—and not just knowledge of specific academic content—are relevant to our students' capacity to make a meaningful and favorable difference in their future world. The phrase "soft skills" is often used to describe aspects of individual emotional IQ—the degree to which individuals manifest skills in knowing themselves and relating with others.

Relational skills—and not just knowledge of specific academic content—are relevant to our students' capacity to make a meaningful and favorable difference in their future world.

Peggy Klaus, professional trainer and recruiter, is all about soft skills. In her book *The Truth About Soft Skills: Workplace Lessons Smart People Wish They'd Learned Sooner*, Klaus notes that shortcomings in social, communication, and self-management skills, not deficits in technical knowledge, are usually what limit or kill a person's career. A recruiter I met at the Association of Career and Technical Education conference I recently presented at echoed the sentiment.

"We get tons of applications from young men and women who look great on paper," he told me.

> We bring them in, we interview them, and then we realize pretty quickly that they have very little clue

how to interact appropriately with other people. If it comes down to choosing between a candidate who has good interpersonal skills but lacks experience versus a candidate with all the technical knowledge but is interpersonally clueless, we'll hire the first candidate every time.

> *By modeling effective soft skills, a teacher creates the kind of effective and safe relational environment necessary to facilitate learning of any academic content.*

The importance of soft skills is not just about preparing students for future opportunity, though. There are here-and-now implications. By modeling effective soft skills, a teacher creates the kind of effective and safe relational environment necessary to facilitate learning of any academic content.

What Is Normal Versus What Is Healthy

We see that research has confirmed what we've already known: healthy relationships are an essential element of the learning process, and effective interpersonal skills go a long way in paving the way for future professional success. That's great and all, but for those of us who were raised in chaotic, unpredictable family-of-origin environments, healthy interpersonal interaction may not feel natural or intuitive. In fact, what we may assume is quite normal actually may be unhealthy. *Never trust anyone. Never depend on anyone. Always keep your guard up. Always strike first.* Those were beliefs I held that did not begin to become undone in me until I was well into my late twenties and many sessions into my own therapy.

My developing the capacity to initiate and sustain healthy relationships was not just about identifying errors in my thinking, but also about actually practicing new skills: *I am choosing to let you help me. I am choosing to be honest with you about what I am thinking and feeling.* It felt awkward at first, but I am grateful that I persevered. Imagine where we would all be today if we gave up on trying to drive a car after the first try because it felt awkward or unnatural. Your self-awareness, your ability to explore your own internal relational landscape is paramount to your ability to initiate and sustain healthy relationships with those around you. Ask yourself: is my normal also healthy?

Generally speaking, most would agree that a healthy relationship is characterized by the following:

- Trust: We can rely and depend on each other.
- Respect: We will give each other our absolute best work.
- Harmony: We will change to accommodate each other when necessary.
- Awareness: We will pay adequate attention to each other.
- Communication: We will openly exchange thoughts and feelings.
- Resilience: We will increase our capacity to recover quickly from setbacks.
- Curiosity: We will seek to know more about each other and the world we share.
- Authenticity: We will be truthful and transparent with each other.
- Boundaries: I am me, you are you, and this is what is and is not acceptable between us.

Many believe that a distinguishing characteristic of a healthy relationship is the absence of conflict. Not true. The healthy relationship begins with the premise that the other person is a good person who makes mistakes. In conflict, then, the starting point is curiosity—not judgment or fear—about why the other made a particular decision. We are being formed continually as we connect with others, and a healthy relationship acknowledges that process of being formed, with a stability and openness to be changed. Further, we extend patience for ourselves and for the other throughout that process. For example, there may be moments when a co-teacher, student, or parent says something incredibly offensive to me; in a healthy relationship, I see this as a place for dialogue of how I have been impacted, rather than an impediment to any further relationship of authenticity or justification to lash out in vengeance.

Even as you read through these descriptors, you're probably already thinking of people in your professional life who feel healthy this way. This is the colleague that is authentically invested in your wellbeing and success as an educator. This is the student who confides in you with her deepest struggles. This is the parent who makes a point of thanking you, regularly, for your investment in their child.

Characteristics of Unhealthy Relationships

We might characterize unhealthy relationships by corollary: unhealthy relationships lack trust, respect, harmony, awareness, communication, resilience, curiosity, authenticity and boundaries. While healthy relationships vitalize (and revitalize) us, unhealthy relationships steal physical and emotional life from us.

Generally speaking, healthy relationships fail to develop or eventually stall or sour for one of two reasons. The first reason is a lack of skills. We cannot implement what we have not been taught; the more time we spend with another person, the more our relational skillset will be tapped. So, interacting with most people for brief periods does not require an extensive relational skill set. But think about how much time you spend on your campus and all the different personality types you encounter on a daily basis among your colleagues, your students and parents.

The second reason healthy relationships fail to develop or eventually sour is a lack of desire. Even when we know what to do, we are faced each day with the question of whether we want healthy relationships enough to invest the resources—the time and the physical and emotional energy—to earn the desired outcome. The investment is particularly difficult if we've attempted to make the investment before in our lives, only to be hurt or otherwise mistreated by the other.

Again, my bet is that you are thinking of people in your life who feel unhealthy this way. "Life-suckers," I call them. This is the colleague who is utterly committed to his bitterness and is known for his habit of slandering other faculty, both privately and publicly. This is the student who violates your physical space and reverts to verbal abuse to manipulate and intimidate others. This is the absentee parent who insists that her child's academic and behavioral difficulties are a direct result and entirely the product of your incompetence as an educator.

We Are Here to Help You

After having conducted staff development and presented at conferences to educators across the country, Jeremy and I began to talk. How do we take this idea of building effective relationships from theory to practice? We knew up front that we did not want to write a book on behavior management or classroom interventions. Those books already exist in abundance.

Could we, as mental health care providers, create a practical guide for educators to position themselves to be most poised to create and sustain the kinds of relationships that would make a difference? We believed we could, but we also knew very well that building and maintaining healthy relationships can be an incredibly complex process—a dance between the interaction of our personalities, histories, fears, skills, and personal development and the same interaction of the other person involved. How could we begin to address the issue for a classroom teacher in a book that wasn't six inches thick?

Jeremy's wife, Jenny, has been an educator for over a decade, and as she overheard us beginning the conversation of this book and how we might step into this question, her input stuck with us:

> I am sure that all the research on why effective relationships are important is really great, but I am a

teacher with a lot on my plate. I think for most of us
as educators, we don't want someone to come in and
waste our time. Back up what you write, but get to
brass tacks quickly and just tell us what we need to
be doing.

She said that in her teacher voice, and it put the fear of God
in us, so we worked out a straightforward text. We identified
four key themes that have emerged in our work with educators in schools and clients in our private practice. It is important for us to note on the outset that a primary philosophical
underpinning in our approach to relationships is a focus on the
internal. What that means is that we believe we reach a place of
greater personal power when we focus on those internal variables that we can control versus those internal variables that
we cannot. And to the degree that external educational variables can be controlled (insofar as they relate to relationship-
building), again, we believe helpful books already exist in
abundance.

As I noted in *The Power of a Teacher*, the average classroom teacher or campus-level administrator has relatively
little control over many policies that impact the day-to-day
realities on any given campus. If you as an educator feel
frustrated and disempowered by that reality, we don't blame
you; we probably would be a bit concerned if you *didn't* feel
that way. Our hope is that the focus and presentation of
the material in this book will provide you with a format to
build relationships while focusing on variables that you can
control.

The idea was to present a format that would guide the
reader through four questions that are foundational to
relationship-building in any context; these four questions
invoke the practices of reflecting, directing, connecting, and
protecting. We'll go into much more detail in subsequent chap-
ters about the implications for each practice, and we'll offer you
practical exercises to give you insight into yourself and practical changes you can make where necessary. But for now, what
follows is an overview of the four practices.

Reflecting: Why Am I Here?

If I have not linked what I'm doing on a daily basis on my campus with my core values (by practicing the skill of reflecting on my identity and calling), it is unlikely that I will understand my role as an educator as anything more than a job, which is simply a basic agreement to exchange labor for a paycheck. In the job model, I will tend to default to offering my employer the minimum amount of my effort in exchange for my established pay rate (a psychological mechanism that allows me to feel that I am getting the highest wage possible). In this mentality, I am unlikely to be willing to spend the effort required to initiate and sustain impactful relationships with colleagues and students.

If, however, I am operating from a calling model, I understand that what I am doing is much less about my paycheck and much more about my living out why I believe I am on this planet. I call this "finding the right why." When I find the right why, I am committed to spending the resources of my time and energy to build relationships because I understand relationships to be the kinds of investments that offer the maximum return as I live out my calling. This is the identity check: Am I primarily an employee who receives a paycheck from a school district, or am I primarily an individual whose calling is to impact the lives of young men and women, and who chooses to live out that calling in the field of education?

Take away: my being in touch with the right "why" is necessary for my campus-level and classroom-level relationships to thrive; if I don't want to be here, I won't be invested in building healthy relationships. You'll meet Martha, a secondary school teacher I saw in my private practice who felt she was lacking a sense of purpose after four years in the profession and was considering changing vocations; after reflecting on her own life story and having focused, meaningful conversations with tenured colleagues, she found understanding and meaning that allowed her to approach her vocation with renewed vitality and meaning.

Directing: How Do I Manage My Emotions?

Emotions are fuel, like gasoline. Gasoline can be used to power a vehicle that can drive a family on a dream vacation, or it can be used to start a fire that will burn down a family home. To preserve nurturing relationships, then, I must practice the skill of experiencing all emotions and directing emotional fuel wisely. If I spend even an hour on any campus in my professional capacity, I am likely to experience a wide-range of emotions, some of which might be both uncomfortable and intense: anger, anxiety, incompetence, sadness. If I do not give myself permission to experience an emotion (to name an emotion is to claim an emotion), I am repressing and storing emotional energy in my body that will eventually cost me. Further, if I am not mindful of how I manage (e.g., express) my emotions, I may be destroying relationships with my colleagues and students by criticizing, attacking, blaming, passive aggression, or withdrawal. My fluency in experiencing and expressing emotion is closely linked to family-of-origin experiences and to my experiences in interpersonal relationships.

If I am not mindful of how I manage (e.g., express) my emotions, I may be destroying relationships with my colleagues and students by criticizing, attacking, blaming, passive aggression, or withdrawal.

Take away: if I habitually suppress emotion or express emotion in hurtful ways, I undermine my capacity to build healthy relationships; wise and appropriate experience and release of emotional fuel is necessary for relationships to thrive. You'll meet Ms. Dunn, a secondary school teacher whose capacity to direct was so fine-tuned that she turned the morning Tony became physically and verbally aggressive toward her by 9:06 a.m. into an opportunity to deepen Tony's trust in her.

Connecting: Can I Build a Bridge?

Bridges are about joining, and to be relationally joined I must practice the skill of connecting to my colleagues and students. The river of difference that separates and divides us can be wide and deep, and it can run with strong undercurrents. Our

looks differ. Our speech differs. Our values differ. Our generations differ. Our neighborhoods differ. Much of how I respond
to the relational stress these differences create arises from my
family-of-origin experience—what was modeled for me by my
parents/role models, siblings, and peers. Will I tap the emotional energy that arises within me as I face that which is unfa-
miliar to build a bridge, or will I use that same energy to avoid
and disengage?

If building bridges does not come naturally to me, I probably am known as a task-oriented individual who can get things
done. Perhaps I am someone who lives more in her mind than
in her heart. I may also be known as someone who is less-than-
approachable in conflict, someone who values a final product
over a person.

Take away: we are by nature relational creatures, and building connections across differences is necessary for relationships
to thrive; if I have talked myself out of my need to be connected
to my colleagues, students, and their parents, it is unlikely that
I will do the work necessary to develop healthy relationships.
You'll meet Coach Williams, the middle-school teacher who
had so mastered the art of non-contingent communication that
he was able to connect with the last parent on earth any faculty
on that campus would have thought was capable of a connection (a parent, by the way, of a different ethnic, socioeconomic,
and generational background than Coach Williams).

Protecting: Can I Build a Fence?

Fences are about defining boundaries—what belongs to me and
what does not? As we engage relationships, we will be hurt. To
stay relationally engaged when I know I am continually at risk
of being hurt, I must practice the skills of protecting my mind
and my heart without isolating myself and falling into bitterness and cynicism.

My fence-building skill is closely linked to whether I view
myself as someone worth being treated with love and respect.
If setting boundaries feels uncomfortable for me, I probably
am known as someone who is warm, nurturing, and emotionally accessible. Perhaps I am someone who lives more in her

Setting healthy boundaries is necessary for relationships to thrive; if I have not empowered myself to protect my mind and heart appropriately, it is unlikely that I will be able to maintain healthy relationships or deal effectively with toxic people.

heart than in her mind. I may also be known as someone who avoids conflict and has difficulty enforcing consequences consistently.

Take away: self-protection is a basic human instinct, and setting healthy boundaries is necessary for relationships to thrive; if I have not empowered myself to protect my mind and heart appropriately, it is unlikely that I will be able to maintain healthy relationships or deal effectively with toxic people. You'll meet Kelley, a primary school teacher who gained the respect of her colleagues when she maintained an entirely professional demeanor while setting absolutely firm boundaries with an administrator who had, for years, bullied teachers into submission with his my-way-or-the-highway authoritarian leadership.

The Case of the Teacher Who Exploded

In the spring semester of 2013, I was asked by a campus-level administrator to partner with her and her leadership team to develop strategies that would incorporate a relationship-building ethic into the campus growth plan. The student population was showing a sharp demographic shift; within a period of five years, it had gone from 85 percent middle to upper-middle class Caucasian to 75 percent low-income Latino and African American. The faculty remained predominantly Caucasian, and they were finding themselves "losing control of the campus," as one teacher put it.

Our early discussions focused on reviewing and revamping the school-wide discipline plan. Positive behavior supports were emphasized, and the counselor offered to lead social skills groups for selected students with excessive office referrals. The leadership team initially expressed a fair amount of enthusiasm: surely, revamping the school-wide and classroom discipline plans will help. As the discussion continued, though, concerns were raised, and tension grew.

"There's no doubt we need this," one teacher noted with increased frustration in her voice, "but what are we supposed to do when the supports we're offering don't work? What are we supposed to do when students simply refuse to comply with our requests, and our consequences are not meaningful to them and not shaping behavior?"

"I understand that not every student will respond favorably the first time," another teacher responded, trying to remain positive. "Still, though, this is what we need to do. This is what will be best for the students and our campus in the long run."

"That's easy for us to say now," the teacher shot back, "but it won't be so easy by the time October gets here, and the honeymoon is over, and we're all already starting to feel tired and burned out."

She was loud.

"You are right. This will be difficult. But I think that's why our relationships with the students are so important. If we can build relationships with the students, I believe they will be more inclined to hear us, more inclined to make the kinds of choices we are wanting them to make."

"Relationships with the kids? Are you kidding me? With all the paperwork I have to do? With all the conferences I have to schedule? With all the activities I have to supervise? I don't have time for relationships!" she exploded, slamming her hand on the table.

And there it was. In her anger, she had given voice to the concern that many of the faculty probably had been struggling with for many months: connecting and building relationships with these students was not coming nearly as naturally or easily or fluidly as it had five years ago. The concern she expressed wasn't unique to this campus; in my work with school districts across the country, I have facilitated countless conversations about how ever-changing standards and regulations have forced the educator to shift attention and energy from building relationships to compliance with legal mandates. It is both a truly legitimate concern and a truly unfortunate reality.

Initiating and sustaining healthy relationships requires effort—emotional and mental work (believe it or not, unhealthy relationships require even more). It's easy to wonder where that effort will come from with so many other demands competing for the limited resources of our mind and heart. Our hope is that through the practices of reflecting, directing, connecting, and protecting, you will be empowered to wisely steward your mental and emotional energy. We hope that you will have a greater sense and framework to posture yourself to most readily engage.

In the next chapter, we will explore the practice of reflecting. Have you linked your most meaningful life experiences and values with what you do on your campus on a day-to-day basis? Have you found the right "why"?

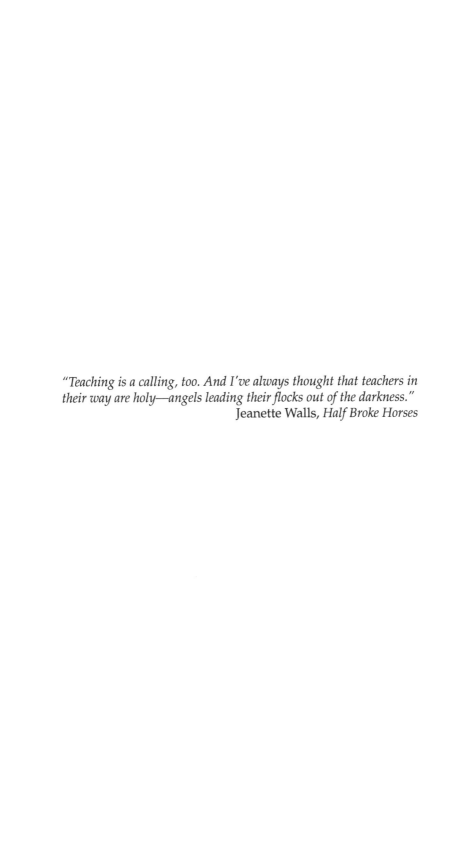

"Teaching is a calling, too. And I've always thought that teachers in their way are holy—angels leading their flocks out of the darkness."
Jeanette Walls, *Half Broke Horses*

2

Reflecting
Why Am I Here?

Two things that make me feel very uncomfortable are heights and electricity. It probably makes sense to you, then, to know that of all the jobs I've had since I started working at the age of fifteen, the one I've liked the least was the job I had in college as an electrician's assistant.

I said it was the job I liked least. That's not entirely accurate. The exact truth is that I hated it. I despised it. I loathed waking up knowing some part of my day would involve being systematically tortured by electricity and a fifteen-foot ladder.

Six months into the job, I knew I was walking around the job site with a bad attitude. I just did not want to be there. I woke up one morning and decided that I was done. Just done. I didn't care if I couldn't pay my rent at the end of the month or my tuition at the end of the semester. I chose those potential stressors over the stress of being an electrician's helper. I showed up for work that morning wearing shorts and flip-flops, walked into the foreman's office, and said, "Mr. Jenks, I'm here to let you know that I'll give you two more weeks, and after that, I'm done."

Mr. Jenks wasn't exactly the warm-fuzzy type, so his response surprised me. I was expecting a chew-out and an invitation to leave immediately.

"I hate to hear that, Adam. You've been a good employee. I'm wondering if there's something we can do to keep you around. I can't offer you more money, but is there a different job site we can consider?"

I thought about it for a moment, and I realized that any job site he sent me to would involve heights (the cat-o'-nine-tails) and electricity (the iron maiden). If only he could triple my salary, give me ten weeks' paid vacation, a company car, and stock options. *Then*, we might have something to discuss here. But he couldn't. The bottom line was that there was nothing he could offer me that would change how I felt about being there. I decided that moment I would be willing to do almost anything else—anything that didn't involve electricity and heights—to earn money for college.

"Thank you, sir," I responded, "but I'm pretty sure I wasn't cut out for this line of work."

Three days later, I took a job waiting tables at a seafood restaurant in the Alamo Heights neighborhood of San Antonio. What a relief: waiting tables required very little direct interaction with electricity or ladders. As I waited tables and paid attention to myself in the process, what I believed about myself for many years was affirmed: I enjoyed interacting with people. As an electrician's assistant, I grew to focus on what I hated about the job (the instruments of torture), but never was aware that my discontent also was rooted in the fact that the job didn't offer what I did enjoy—interaction with a wide variety of people.

My mother did not have a college degree, and she spent most of her life making just above minimum wage; the only concept I had of employment, thus, was the idea that you were lucky if you had a job, and luckier still if it happened to be one that paid most of your bills. There was never talk of careers or callings. It was all about just getting by.

Something about that ideology, though, never really sat well with me. The employment experience I had as the electrician's helper and, subsequently, as a waiter, was my first realization that it was important for me to link what I believe, what I enjoy, and who I am with what I do on a day-to-day basis.

If I'm not invested at a very deep, very fundamental level—beyond just the paycheck—in how I am spending each day, I will not and cannot be engaged deeply. Well, I take that back. I

If I'm not invested at a very deep, very fundamental level—beyond just the paycheck—in how I am spending each day, I will not and cannot be engaged deeply.

probably will be engaged, but engaged in a very non-productive, resentful posture. If I am in that non-productive, resentful place as an educator, my sense of resentment will spread to my colleagues, my students and their parents, essentially creating a dynamic in which my entire professional world will have to pay rent on my sense of dissatisfaction with life. And if I am in that place, there is no external change—no academic or behavioral intervention, no organizational restructuring, no pay raise—that will breathe life into me. That place is the place where souls go to get crushed.

What are your thoughts and feelings about your role as an educator? Let me be more specific: What are your thoughts as you enter and exit the parking lot on your campus? How do you feel when you walk onto your campus? How do you feel when you interact with your colleagues? Your students? Their parents? What are your thoughts as you prepare your lesson plans? Do you think and feel about those things the way I thought and felt about ladders and electricity, or does something deep within you, even in the occasional monotony of it all, give you a quiet affirmation that you really are where you need to be?

What I am getting at here is the concept of calling, which boils down to the why—*why are we doing what we are doing?* Finding the right why, through reflection, is important, because without it, we are unlikely to have the fortitude to persevere through the struggles and trials that are inherent in any vocation, particularly those in the field of education. By definition, we are passionate about our values, and the idea is that in linking our deepest values with what we do on a daily basis, we create access to a fuel source that is pure enough and vast enough to sustain us over the course of our life in our vocation.

Jobs, Careers, and Callings

To better understand how our attitudes impact our approach to our profession, we are wise to understand the differences between a job, a career, and a calling. We often use these words interchangeably in our conversational language, but they can represent significantly different ideas.

A job is simply a basic agreement to swap labor for a paycheck. This can happen on any scale: yes, I will cook food for an hourly wage of $7.50. Or, yes, I will trade real estate futures for an hourly wage of $750.00. In job mode, the end game is about money, and my underlying motive is to increase the amount of money I am receiving in exchange for the same sixty minutes of my life force.

A career is a job with advancement opportunities. Yes, I will cook food for an hourly wage of $7.50 now because I know that in six months, I will have the opportunity to manage the kitchen for an hourly wage of $10.50. Then, in a year, I will have the opportunity to manage the entire restaurant for an hourly wage of $16.50. As with a job, the end game is about maximizing my return. In career mode, though, I'm wanting to maximize not only the amount of money I am trading for sixty minutes of my life force, but also my responsibility and choices. There is more pay off here.

> Unlike a job or a career, though, a calling is what we do for the intrinsic value of the activity itself. In other words, the activity itself offers the primary reward.

Unlike a job or a career, though, a calling is what we do for the intrinsic value of the activity itself. In other words, the activity itself offers the primary reward; financial return and potential advancement opportunity are simply side-effects.

My intention is not to portray a calling as a morally superior venture than a job or a career. We need jobs because we need paychecks; I place a high value on having a paycheck to meet my family's needs for food, clothing, and shelter. We need careers because we need advancement opportunities. I also place a high value on being able to increase my capacity to steward increased responsibility. I truly am thankful for both jobs and careers. As I mentioned above, though, without the calling piece of it—without finding the right why—I have, at best, limited myself in my capacity to truly flourish in my vocational endeavors, and, at worst, set myself up for a fairly significant existential breakdown. That existential breakdown likely will occur in the parking lot of my campus, one cold morning as I sit in my warm car, wondering whether I really want to open my car door and walk the two hundred yards into the building. *"They don't pay me enough to put up with this,"* I will tell myself. "I should get my license to sell real estate."

In distinguishing among jobs, careers, and callings, we should remember that every vocation will have job moments, career moments, and calling moments. My work as a psychologist feels like a job when I am on the phone with an insurance company trying to secure preauthorization to treat a patient or following up on a claim I've submitted. I've spent as much as forty-five minutes being looped through automated voice cues, only to be placed on hold, only to be disconnected. It doesn't crush my entire soul when that happens, but it steps on the little toe of my soul, and I don't like it; it feels like I'm just swapping my time for an amount of money.

I have career moments as a psychologist when I think about how we can grow our practice. Can we offer more pre-marital counseling services? Can we reach out to more school districts to offer professional development for teachers around building effective relationships? Can we collaborate with local non-profit organizations to provide free training and support for parents who have adopted children with special needs? Those moments, as you can imagine, are much more exciting and fulfilling than the job moments.

When I think about the peaks and valleys of my life and the role educators played in those times, I know my calling: it is to encourage and equip educators in their calling with students. I have calling moments when I am standing in front of a group of educators reminding them that what they do matters and giving them practical steps to care for themselves. Those moments, for me, are their own rewards. Those moments resonate with something deep within me, and each time, they help me better understand how and why I experienced the early life I did and, later, the educational and training that I have.

Typically, the frequency, intensity, and duration of a vocation's job moments will outnumber the career moments and calling moments. In fact, we may sometimes experience weeks or many months as nothing more than a series of job moments. Given that, it is so important for us to document the calling moments so we never lose sight of our right why.

Teaching might feel like a job when the copy machine jams for the sixth time in a day, making you late for the parent conference you have with the parent that is angry that you haven't transformed their oppositional child into a potential Nobel Laureate. Teaching may feel like a career after you've oriented yourself into your role and begun to take on more responsibility—department chair, for example. When does teaching feel like a calling for you? If you're having difficulty answering that question, our hope is that the exercise at the end of the chapter will help you find clarity.

A Bit More About Calling

When most people consider the meaning of the word calling, they probably think of it in a religious or spiritual context; calling connotes an image of Moses and a burning bush—a higher power meeting us to give us a specific instruction on how to invest our life force. Certainly, calling can include an individual's spirituality. However, in its most broad sense, calling is simply about knowing what we value, and then living out and expressing that value to improve our life and the lives of those with whom we interact on a regular basis. What do I believe to be true about the human experience? Why am I here, on this planet, in this city, in this family, in these relationships, on this campus, in this classroom?

In many ways, calling links our past, present, and future. People with a clear sense of calling often have a clear sense of the driving factors that have shaped the values they carry. As Adam has shared, his route to becoming a psychologist and working with educators in the area of wellbeing is deeply connected to the voices of teachers that spoke value into his life as a student, teachers that carried satisfaction into their work in such a way that it spoke light into the dark places of his childhood.

For me (Jeremy), it is of little wonder to me that I find myself working with children and adolescents, as well as the adults who guide them, after making a promise at the age of ten or eleven that I would not be another adult who forgot what it was like to be a child. That childhood promise was fueled by relationships with adults on both sides—those who had forgotten, leaving me feeling misunderstood and alone, and those who did understand me and helped me to find my potential and strengthened my unique voice.

In other words, our calling is often written in the peaks and valleys of our upbringing—where we have known the greatest harm and the most significant redemption. This doesn't require a religious system. Instead, it is part of being human and having a unique story to share with others. When we understand the peaks and valleys of our upbringing and link them to how we invest our life force each day, we endow each day, each activity, each relationship, each point of contact with a deeper, transcendent meaning.

This linking is the process of finding the right why. Any individual or group, given the right why, is capable of overcoming any obstacle for results even beyond their individual or collective potential. This is what advertising consultant Simon Sinek was getting at—at least in part—in his book *Start With Why: How Great Leaders Inspire Everyone To Take Action*. When I am teaching with a sense of calling, from the right why, I approach the task of building relationships with a resolve to share my passion with my community, to invite others into a collective expression of values—namely the value of impacting the next generation of learners.

Meet Martha

As I reviewed Martha's referral paperwork in my office, her presentation seemed pretty straightforward; she was a twenty-eight-year-old Caucasian female seeking counseling for depression—it was the kind of garden-variety referral we get in our clinic, on average, about four to five times a day. What immediately struck me about Martha's demographic information, though, was her profession: teacher. I called her and scheduled our first session.

When she arrived, I immediately sensed her tension as I greeted her in the waiting room. She was an attractive young woman, but her posture was slouched, and she seemed to walk with a slow, stiff gait as she stood and approached me to shake my hand. She offered a half-hearted smile and made little eye contact.

As we settled into my office, I reviewed my office policy, the limits of confidentiality—all the housekeeping procedures the law requires. Finally, I looked at Martha and asked, "So, what brings you in today?"

She paused. "I'm not sure, really," she said. "I think I'm depressed. I haven't been sleeping well, I seem to have lost my appetite, and it feels like a huge chore just to wake up and get out of bed every day. I'm not really crying a lot or anything like that, but I do have this gnawing feeling that something's not right in my life."

I spent the rest of the session turning the usual stones. Medical issues? No. She had recently undergone a complete physical with a panel of blood work, and the results were unremarkable. Marital issues? No. She and her husband had been happily married for four years, and they were talking about having a child. Family-of-origin issues? No. Her mother passed away when she was in high school, but she seemed to have grieved the loss appropriately, and she maintained a healthy relationship with her father and siblings. No in-law issues, either.

As we closed the session, I was at something of a loss. I didn't feel like I had identified any potential source or cause of her depression, and I was not quite sure how to proceed with a treatment plan. Then, just before we concluded, she offered a clue.

"Oh, yeah," she noted. "I have noticed kind of a pattern over the course of the past two years: the feelings get better at the beginning of the summer, and they get worse in August."

Aha.

We spent the next session exploring her occupation. How did she like her campus? Her administrator? The kids? The parents? As she described the course of the past four years as a teacher, there definitely was a pattern of decreasing satisfaction with her role as an educator.

"I was so excited when I started. I looked forward to show-ing up to my campus every day and being with the kids and the rest of the faculty. Maybe it was just the newness of it all. I don't know. But the further I got into it, the more I began to wonder what I was really doing. Now, I feel like I don't even want to be around anyone on my campus anymore, and I really don't like what I'm becoming. I'm just sort of wondering, 'What is the point of all this?'"

We sat in silence for a few beats.

"Sounds like you're questioning whether you want to con-tinue as a teacher," I offered. "Tell me: why did you enter the profession?"

She thought about it for a moment. "I guess it's because my mom was a teacher."

"Did you think through what a lifetime as an educator would look like for you?" I asked. "I mean, did you ever really consider whether you were cut out for this type of work, what it was all about, and whether it would be meaningful to you?"

"Not really, I guess. I just wanted to get through college and find a job. This seemed to be what made most sense. I saw my mom do it year after year until she passed away. But now that I'm in my fourth year of it, I'm seeing things in the kids, in the parents, and in the system that I never realized went with the territory. Sometimes it really does feel like a beat-down."

"I think I would be depressed, too."

She smiled. Sort of.

"Martha, it sounds like you started off well, but at some point, you lost the passion. I'm wondering if it might be help-ful for you to explore your sense of purpose in your profession. We all go through ups and downs, rich seasons and lean sea-sons, in what we do. Maybe if you spend some time exploring your sense of calling, you might be better equipped to decide whether a change in vocation is the right solution for you. We tend to live our best lives when we live deliberately, knowing at a deep level *why* we are doing what we are doing."

She thought about it for a moment. "Maybe you're right."

I gave Martha homework. She was to begin by charting out her life map. What were the highs? What were the lows? Who were the heroes? Who were the villains? Then, what did her life's

narrative, in combination with her personality, strengths, and
weaknesses, suggest about who she was and what she wanted to
do with her life? Then, I asked Martha to interview senior faculty
on her campus. I warned her, though: make sure it's no one from
the angry, bitter, resentful crowd that has been in education since
the Kennedy administration. That will only make your depression worse, I told her. Instead, find someone who has been at it
for a while and still moves with a purpose, still shows up with
something to offer, and still gets excited about learning.

One thing I love about working with teachers in my private
practice is that they tend to be compulsive about completing
homework when I assign it. Martha was no exception. It didn't
happen overnight, but over the course of the next several sessions, Martha began to recount to me her findings. As she traced
back over her life, she realized that her mother was her hero, a
reality that was underscored as she spent time with senior colleagues on her campus whom she admired. In the end, Martha
was able to understand her role as an educator as her living out
the legacy her mother had left her.

My work with Martha was mostly about helping her find a
deeper purpose—the right why. But it was not totally about that.
We also discovered some peripheral issues related to the loss
of her mother. Being in a school every day reminded her of her
mother, and we realized she still had more grieving to do, particularly as she and her husband were considering starting a family.

Identifying Your Right Why

We have created an exercise for you to complete, and the idea
is to provide you with a format to begin to link the peaks and
valleys of your history to what excites and animates you today,
and then to link that with your role as an educator. We have
guided educators through this exercise on campuses across the
country, and we have included below responses from seven ran-
domly selected teachers and administrators; their responses are
in order across all sentences (in other words, the first response
on each sentence is from person one, the second response on
each sentence is from person two, etc.). As you read through
these responses, we hope you will gain a sense of how deeply

personal the respondents have been; I believe it is precisely because they have been so raw and honest in their responses that they have been able to generate such deeply meaningful personal mission statements. They have found their right why. It may be helpful to you to read their responses before you engage the task yourself.

This exercise is called a sentence completion task. We have provided specific sentence stems that are intended to focus your thinking on experiences that are likely to have the most direct link to your vocation as an educator. Your task is to read the stem and complete the sentence as honestly as possible. Afterward, you will reflect on the completed sentences to look for themes or ideas that might inform your personal mission statement as an educator. Here are the directions: First, read through all the sentences. Then, read through the sample responses we have collected from educators across the country. Finally, after you've gained a sense of what the sentence stems are getting at (particularly the very last two), go back and complete the sentences for yourself.

Identifying My Calling: A Sentence Completion Exercise

The Past

1. My best memory of school is _____.
2. My worst memory of school is _____.
3. When I was a student, my social life was _____.
4. Most of my classmates thought I was _____.
5. Most of my teachers thought I was _____.
6. The hardest part of being a student for me was
   _____.
7. My favorite teachers always _____.
8. My favorite teachers never_____.
9. When I was young, I never wanted to _____.
10. When I was young, I always hoped I would _____.

The Present

1. People who are not educators will never understand
   _____.

2. I feel most sure that I am in the right vocation when
   _____.

3. I feel least sure that I am in the right vocation when
   _____.

4. I wish someone would have told me before I started
   my vocation as an educator that _____.

5. My greatest strength as an educator probably is __
   _____.

6. My greatest weakness as an educator probably is
   _____.

7. Part of my past that really helps me as an educator
   is _____.

8. Part of my past that really limits me as an educator is
   _____.

9. Even if I'm not convinced that I should be an educator, I am so glad that I am not a _____.

10. I want to be a part of a faculty that _____.

The Future

1. My advice to a first-year teacher would be _____.

2. I will become a more effective educator each year by
   _____.

3. Many years from now, I hope to be remembered by
   my colleagues as _____.

4. Many years from now, I hope to be remembered by
   my students as _____.

5. Many years from now, I hope to be remembered by
   parents as _____.

6. I believe I can say that my life as an educator will have been well-spent if _____.

7. I would regret retiring from a lifetime in education and looking back to see that _____.

Two More Sentences: Creating Your Personal Mission Statement

As you review your sentence completion, can you identify themes? How is your passion as an educator fueled by your early experiences—both pleasant and unpleasant—in school? How is who you are as an educator linked to what you experienced with the heroes and villains in your life?

As you reflect on these questions, consider the final two sentence stems below. What we'd like you to do is complete both statements, which will become your personal mission statements as an educator. The "I am an educator because . . . " statement is a tool to concisely frame your right why. The "Because I am an educator . . . " statement is a tool to concisely frame your hope for the impact you would like to make as an educator.

I am an educator because _____.

Because I am an educator, _____.

Sample Sentence Completion Responses
The Past

My best memory of school is . . .

a junior high teacher who did things differently in her classroom . . . always looked forward to her class because I never knew what to expect!

the friends that I made and still have today, including my teachers.

in twelfth grade, my Trig teacher gave me a challenge—to prove the number "e"; I brought it back to him every day for three weeks before I solved it, and I loved every minute of it.

when I was selected to the homecoming court my senior year—I was surprised!

first grade—I loved my teacher and learning all the vowel sounds.

it's hard to name one because I really enjoyed all of school.

high school marching band.

My worst memory of school is . . .

being leveled by color in reading, we had to work our way through (boring for an already avid reader).

my fourth-grade teacher who said I would be lucky to finish high school and that I was too dumb to go to college.

in fifth grade when I realized I would have to "tutor" my classmates for most of the year.

when I was made fun of and called out in front of my class by my first-grade teacher for plagiarizing my book report.

being picked on by a boy.

first grade, because I had a very strict, unfriendly teacher.

the elementary school playground.

When I was a student, my social life was . . .

good, but I loved school and was studious . . . never got in trouble and always wanted to please my teachers.

good—I had a lot of friends.

about survival. I was one of three kids [of my race] in the school.

quiet.

good—I had a small group of close friends.

limited.

limited to a small group of people, but fulfilling.

Most of my classmates thought I was . . .

smart, a good student, and bossy.

a nice person.

weird.

nice.

smart and quiet.

snobby, but I was just insecure.

an average, nice kid.

Most of my teachers thought I was . . .

studious, hard-working, showed leadership.

a good student, but a chatterbox.

the "good girl."

good and quiet.

smart and quiet.

a hard-working, good student.

a good student who talked a bit too much.

The hardest part of being a student for me was . . .

not always having the social life I wanted . . . took all accelerated classes and had a pretty full schedule.

doing my work instead of spending all the time talking to my friends.

knowing that no one would ever understand my Obsessive Compulsive Disorder.

not ever wanting to be called out or asked to read.

explaining to my friends about my father's death in the second grade.

when I missed a lot of school because I was sick.

nothing, really.

My favorite teachers always . . .

> *made learning fun, changed it up often, challenged me.*
>
> *encouraged me and made the class interesting.*
>
> *allowed me to go as far as I wanted in any given subject.*
>
> *smiled and talked to me . . . she said my name a lot when she talked to me.*
>
> *helped us learn in a fun way.*
>
> *encouraged and challenged me.*
>
> *challenged me to think.*

My favorite teachers never . . .

> *sat at their desks.*
>
> *put me down or made me feel bad because they always encouraged me to do my best.*
>
> *told me what I wanted to try was silly or a waste of time.*
>
> *talked down to me or acted bothered to answer my questions.*
>
> *singled out anyone who was struggling.*
>
> *yelled at us.*
>
> *belittled me.*

When I was young, I never wanted to . . .

> *miss school.*
>
> *be a teacher.*
>
> *be pointed out . . . I preferred to sit in the back of the room and finish quickly so I could read.*
>
> *disappoint my parents.*
>
> *be a teacher.*
>
> *upset people or be in trouble.*
>
> *disappoint my parents.*

When I was young, I always hoped I would . . .

be a teacher.

be a nurse, until I found out it involved blood.

be athletic (I was a geeky kid with glasses and asthma).

have a family.

own my own business.

be a doctor (but then found teaching and fell in love with it).

get a college degree.

The Present

People who are not educators will never understand . . .

all the things teachers do for their students . . . the time and money they spend is unbelievable.

all the acronyms, behaviors, and why I continue to do the job day after day, year after year.

the emotional or physical toll it takes . . . it leaves you completely drained.

the emotional drain it takes on you to care for so many people.

how much work it is to be a teacher.

how hard the job is, how much time and emotional energy it requires.

the stress of teaching and under-appreciation of teachers.

I feel most sure that I am in the right vocation when . . .

a student who is struggling academically or behaviorally begins to responding to intervention and is proud of themselves.

I catch myself smiling as I leave each day to go to school and I look forward to school starting.

I see the "light" come on in a student's eyes—then I know the missed lunches and late nights are worth it.

my students (especially the difficult ones) want to be near me.

I hear from former students.

when my students have that "aha" moment, and I know that I am part of it, I feel like I am growing personally.

I feel least sure that I am in the right vocation when . . .

the "red tape" keeps me from helping kids who really need help.

I see how my students perform poorly on a test over material I thought they understood.

I do everything I can think of (and that's quite a bit), but the student or their parents are still belligerent and rude.

my students perform poorly on a test that I thought they would do well on because I taught them so many different ways.

I have to deal with classroom management issues.

my stress level goes through the roof.

I feel stagnant and unappreciated.

I wish someone would have told me before I started my vocation as an educator that . . .

politics and legalities play such a huge part of our business.

it would be as rewarding and entertaining as it is each day.

the trend in education is moving away from the respect and discipline a teacher deserves and more towards a PR-style of teaching.

parents can be so different [in their parenting approach] than the way my husband and I parent.

[nothing], I was pretty well prepared.

it is important to set boundaries because otherwise your job can take over your life.

the teachers, who have the most contact with the students, make the fewest decisions about how to teach them.

My greatest strength as an educator probably is . . .

> *my willingness to do whatever I need to so my students are successful.*
>
> *being flexible and understanding that everyone is an individual and not something that fits into the same mold year after year.*
>
> *being able to empathize with students, because I remember what it was like to be picked on, tripped in the hallway or jumped in the bathroom.*
>
> *knowing I have the opportunity/responsibility to influence each child I come in contact with to be the best possible version of themselves.*
>
> *my discipline and my determination to do my best.*
>
> *my work ethic and my love for the students.*
>
> *my ability to form relationships with my students.*

My greatest weakness as an educator probably is . . .

> *my tendency to spread myself too thin.*
>
> *the lack of confidence I feel around my peers because I have not had education classes like they did in college (I was an alternatively certified teacher with an accounting degree).*
>
> *my frustration with a kid who says "I don't get it" [and shuts down].*
>
> *that I often feel frustrated and overwhelmed that I do not reach every student in the one year I have with them.*
>
> *wanting to help the kids succeed more than they want success for themselves.*
>
> *how hard it is for me to say no.*
>
> *my inability to cope with the stress.*

Part of my past that really helps me as an educator is . . .

> *having taught secondary, junior high school and elementary has helped me understand "the big picture."*

that I remember what it was like as a student to be told by a
teacher that I am dumb and stupid.

my memories of what I loved from my teachers and thinking about
how I can have that same effect on my students.

the feelings I had toward the teachers I liked and disliked . . . I
pretend to be Mrs. Bayne, my ninth-grade science teacher.

both my parents were educators.

[no answer].

my training as a youth minister.

Part of my past that really limits me as an educator is . . .

having grown up in a very small district as a child and now working in a huge district.

having worked in the past for administrators who entered the new
school years with a list of teachers they wanted to leave their
campus at the end of the year.

having a tendency to "re-live" some of my own past issues in the
classroom.

[focusing] on all the things that limited me.

[no answer].

my perfectionist nature.

[no answer].

Even if I'm not convinced that I should be an educator, I am so
glad that I am not a . . .

lawyer!

president of a large corporation.

sales rep.

stay-at-home mom, because it's better for all of us when I have
something that is all my own.

nine-to-five worker.

garbage man?

plumber. I hate plumbing.

I want to be a part of a faculty that . . .

> *cares about one another, teaches to the whole child, and believes in the value of hard work.*
>
> *shares information and believes in working together to create a wonderful working environment.*
>
> *does what's best for kids no matter what it costs or how hard it is.*
>
> *really has each other to lean on (I feel that way about my [current campus] family.)*
>
> *shows concern for each other.*
>
> *works together to problem solve and challenge each other in a fun, supportive environment.*
>
> *appreciates each other.*

The Future

My advice to a first-year teacher would be . . .

> *learn all you can about different learning styles and classroom management; be willing to put in the overtime.*
>
> *don't be afraid to ask questions, to ask for help from your peers/ principals, and remember they were first-year teachers once, too. You will survive this.*
>
> *expect to work harder than you ever thought possible [and] give yourself permission to be wrong and admit to the kids when you are.*
>
> *learn what not to do just as much as what to do.*
>
> *stay organized! And then get the parents on your side.*
>
> *hang in there! It is REALLY hard (and very normal to want to quit), but it is worth it.*
>
> *hang on. It will get better in year two.*

I will become a more effective educator each year by . . .

> *networking, reading, reflecting, collaborating.*
>
> *always learning and trying something new.*

continuing my own education and being sure that I "sharpen the saw" in my own life so that I can lift them up when they need it.

evaluating myself and allowing students to evaluate me.

reading and continuing to attend professional development activities.

reflecting and adapting to my students' needs.

using new ideas and methods.

Many years from now, I hope to be remembered by my colleagues as . . .

someone who was good to work for and who would go the extra mile for her teachers and her students.

a good teacher and a helpful, caring person that they felt lucky to have worked with.

someone who was a team player and had a true love of teaching.

a helpful friend who they enjoyed being around.

a dedicated teacher who always went the extra mile.

someone who was willing to offer help, and a team player.

helpful.

Many years from now, I hope to be remembered by my students as . . .

someone who they KNEW cared about them.

a teacher who taught them something they could use in life.

someone who loved her job and passed the love of [her field] onto her students.

a person they felt safe and important with.

a fun, friendly teacher that pushed them to succeed.

someone who inspired them to learn and to be better people.

a teacher who loved them.

Many years from now, I hope to be remembered by parents as . . .

> *someone who cared about their kids and their school.*
>
> *a teacher who was concerned about their students as well as a teacher who taught their children well.*
>
> *someone who did everything possible to give their children passion for [the subject].*
>
> *a teacher who really got to know and help their child.*
>
> *a teacher who expected the best from every student.*
>
> *someone who cared about their children.*
>
> *a teacher who influenced their child.*

I believe I can say that my life as an educator will have been well-spent if . . .

> *I truly made an impact on kids and how they see themselves.*
>
> *I had started teaching earlier in life than I did, instead of waiting to teach as a second career.*
>
> *I brought the smallest bit of joy into [the students' lives] through my subject.*
>
> *my students look back and wonder "would Ms. E be proud or disappointed in me for what I am about to do?"*
>
> *my students come back and see me at school—which they do!*
>
> *inspire my students to be life-long learners.*
>
> *I help prepare future citizens.*

I would regret retiring from a lifetime in education and looking back to see that . . .

> *I didn't try new things and make a difference!*
>
> *I had become stagnant in my teaching and did not move forward with the times.*

I was no better than the teachers I despised.

the connections I thought I made with students were not meaningful.

[nothing].

our public education system is a mess.

I did not better my community.

Personal Mission Statement

I am an educator because . . .

I was influenced by good educators, and I believe in the power of the profession.

I saw the simple skills that had been taught to my younger brother (who has [an intellectual disability]), and I wanted to give to others as teachers had helped my younger brother to help him have a more complete life.

I know I was called to do so.

I have the ability and desire to connect with students and to use the relationship to make them better learners and people.

I love learning and want to foster good learning skills in my students to help promote their success.

I LOVE exciting students about studying the world around them and showing them they are capable of so much more than they think they are.

I want to change lives.

Because I am an educator . . .

I am tired, but content in knowing that what I do matters.

I have had the opportunity to experience the joy and heartache of working with students, and in the end, know that in some small way I have changed their lives.

I spend every ounce of myself when I teach my class [and] I am honest about how I feel and model how an adult makes choices and decisions.

I am responsible for providing a safe environment to help develop good learning and good people.

I must keep up with learning trends and work with students and parents to instill good work habits.

I have the privilege of shaping the lives of young people and of learning with them.

I hope my students will have better lives.

After you've finished the sentence completion exercise and created your personal mission statement with those last two sentences (*"I am an educator because . . ."* and *"Because I am an educator . . ."*), I encourage you to write your personal mission statement on an 3 × 5 index card and keep multiple copies with you, maybe one on your desk and one in some other location that is a part of your daily routine. Remember, this mission statement is, in some important ways, your antidote when the job moments seem to string together to make job weeks, job months, job semesters and job years. This mission statement has the power to repeatedly bring you back to your right why.

How Reflecting on Calling Impacts Relationships

If I don't want to be on my campus (or, more generally speaking, in education), I am highly unlikely to do the work necessary to build healthy relationships. I will show up to work as late as possible in the morning, and I will leave work as early as possible in the afternoon. I will perceive interaction with others as a burden, and I likely will approach others in a posture of wondering how they can meet my needs and what is in it for me. In other words, my cup always will be half empty.

My colleagues likely will perceive me as detached, disengaged, unapproachable, and unpleasant. My students (especially the younger ones, because no one picks up on emotion like a child) will feel my negative vibe. They will sense that I do not want to be in the classroom, and that I have little interest or capacity in getting to know them. As a result of that relational gap, my students will have very low desire to please me or to respond favorably to my direction because, they will reason, if I am not invested, why should they be? Finally, when parents do reach out to me, they, too, immediately will sense the "Do Not Disturb" vibe I give off, which, in turn, will render them mistrusting of me and most likely to assume the very worst about what they know—directly or indirectly. If I continue in that posture for too long, I am likely to develop a toxic emotional life that will, in turn, further poison my interaction with everyone with whom I have contact on a daily basis.

When I know my calling, however, I am connected to the right *why*, I will perceive colleagues as collaborators in my journey. In that collaborative mindset, my colleagues and I become resources to each other as we grow in our capacity to engage learners with increased efficacy and result. We share excitement, frustration, hope, concerns, give each other difficult feedback and deep affirmation. When I know my right *why*, I will be invested in getting to know my students, because I will be continually reminded that they are a central focus of my calling. I will enter into and invest in their lives as much as possible, knowing that the return on my investment has the potential to pay for generations. I will understand my students' parents as primary resources in their lives, and I will seek to incorporate and empower them in the education process.

> **When I know my right *why*, I will be invested in getting to know my students, because I will be continually reminded that they are a central focus of my calling.**

I'll conclude this chapter with a final underscore of the importance of living from the right why. I've been on my own since I left high school at eighteen (and in some ways, well before then), and I have wanted to be the kind of person that lived with no regrets, especially since I had so many regrets about what I experienced in life before the age of eighteen. If I am fortunate enough to live another forty years, I hope to look back and echo the words of Henry David Thoreau:

> I went to the woods because I wished to live deliberately, to front only the essential facts of life, and see if I could not learn what it had to teach, and not, when I came to die, discover that I had not lived. I did not

wish to live what was not life, living is so dear; nor did I wish to practise resignation, unless it was quite necessary. I wanted to live deep and suck out all the marrow of life . . .

Here is a point of reference for you: imagine that human history spanned a twenty-four-hour block, say, from one midnight to the next. The last *fourteen minutes* of the last of those twenty-four hours represents the 2,000 or so years since the time of Christ. Now, let's move more specifically to the context of the individual lifespan. Speaking in statistical averages, we will be alive 30,000 days. Since we will spend one-third of that time asleep, we are left with a waking lifespan of 20,000 days to actually live our calling. If you are relatively young and just out of college, you have already burned about one-fourth of them, leaving you with 15,000. If you are middle-aged, like me, you can rest assured that you have more yesterdays than tomorrows.

The point here is not to depress you, but to remind you that our lives—even when we are fortunate enough to get the full eighty-five or so years—are vapors. Time is now. If you haven't already established why you are choosing to invest your life force in any given venture, you owe it to yourself to do so now.

Key Point Summary

- ♦ Calling categorically differs from job and career. We need jobs and careers, but without the calling piece, we are unlikely to do the work necessary to establish healthy relationships.

- ♦ Understanding our calling is about finding our right why.

- ♦ Identifying my calling does not necessarily require a religious system.

- ♦ Calling—what animates and brings me to life— usually is linked to the peaks and valleys of my life's experiences.

"If your emotional abilities aren't in hand, if you don't have self-awareness, if you are not able to manage your distressing emotions, if you can't have empathy and have effective relationships, then no matter how smart you are, you are not going to get very far."

Daniel Goleman

3

Directing
Can I Manage My Emotions?

Emotions can be defined many ways, but at their core, emotions are biochemical responses to internal and external stimuli. Emotions—these biochemical reactions—are energy, just like the food we eat, and we metabolize both forms of energy similarly. Some of the food energy I consume will be burned throughout the day to power my body. Some of it will be stored (for me, usually around my midsection). What is not burned or stored—the rest of it—will be, shall we say, "evacuated." Our bodies will do with the fuel of emotional energy the same thing they do with the fuel of food. Emotions arise in response to internal (e.g., thoughts or memories) or external (e.g., sensory) experiences, and as these emotions arise to produce this biochemical fuel, our bodies either will burn it to power themselves, or will store it, in a joint, muscle or organ.

Just as stuffing our bodies with excessive food/fuel results in physical dis-ease, stuffing (or disregarding or minimizing or denying) our emotions results in psychological dis-ease. The relationship actually is interactive: physical illness can deplete my emotional functioning, and emotional illness can have a physical effect. The process of developing physical symptoms that are rooted in emotion is called somatization, which is the body's way of signaling a dashboard light to let those of us who are prone to denial and minimizing and disregarding emotion that something inside needs attention.

The capacity to effectively process emotion is referred to as emotional intelligence, including the innate ability to feel, use, communicate, recognize, remember, describe, identify, learn from, manage, understand, and explain emotions. Apart from academic content, teachers also teach social/emotional content by modeling for students appropriate ways to experience and express intense emotions, such as anger and anxiety. Just as a limited understanding of my content area will diminish my capacity to teach it, so too will having limited emotional intelligence decrease my capacity to teach appropriate emotional regulation. The good news is that all emotions—even the most powerful and uncomfortable ones—can be experienced and expressed in ways that are life-giving and in ways that build connection and intimacy.

Emotional Constipation

Experiencing emotion is a fairly straightforward process: to name it is to claim it. To say, "I feel sad" is to acknowledge the presence of the feeling. Until I use language to name the feeling, I am stuck in the position of having emotional energy locked inside me, perhaps without my own awareness that the emotional energy is present or how the energy might be affecting me.

While that process of naming emotions is straightforward, it may not be particularly easy. Let me use the emotion of anger— often a problematic emotion—to illustrate. If I grew up in a family in which someone habitually used the fuel of anger to physically or emotionally harm me or someone I care about, I likely developed problematic responses around the emotion of anger. One of two outcomes is most likely: I will either embrace what has been modeled for me and hurt others with the fuel of my anger ("That's perfectly normal behavior," I will reason, based on what was modeled for me), or I will not give myself permission to feel anger and shut off the emotion (thereby guaranteeing that I will never hurt anyone with anger).

Neither option is ideal. The first hurts others. The second hurts me. What I know as a licensed psychologist is that I can say that I don't do anger, but I guarantee anger is doing me. When I develop a pattern of denying or repressing any emotion, it's just a matter of time before the stored up fuel of that emotion in my body becomes toxic. The crisis moment may come in the form of an eventual emotional explosion, a nervous breakdown, digestive problems, chronic pain and inflammation, or any other host of physical problems that are rooted in the repressed emotion. I lose the ability to initiate and sustain sleep, and I generally feel fatigued and run-down.

Further, until that crisis moment comes, I probably will end up expressing my anger with passive aggression ("Oh, that was *your* drawing I accidentally destroyed in the trash? Well, sorry if you got your feelings hurt"). Repressing emotion diminishes the quality of my life. When I deny my emotions, I deny my experience and I negate myself. In essence, I live a less-than-authentic life.

I used anger as an example because it is the most commonly problematic emotion. The dynamic I just illustrated, though, can be true of any emotion: sadness, confusion—even happiness. I grew up in a single parent, low income home. My mother was under constant stress for a variety of reasons, and one message I internalized growing up was "It's not okay to be happy." Life is a beat-down, I was taught, and there is no room for happiness, because if misery is not here right now, rest assured, it is always just around the corner. Part of my maladaptive response to the life-is-a-beat-down mentality was to develop an insane work ethic (if I just work my fingers to the bone, then I might make enough money to protect myself from life's cruelty). I am only now, in my middle age, beginning to give myself freedom to be happy. My wife would argue—quite convincingly—that I'm not quite there yet; as I write these words, my family and I are on a five-day cruise, and I have secluded myself on a remote part of the ship for six hours to finish this chapter. It seems I still feel compelled to mix duty with pleasure to appease my guilt.

Experiencing Emotions

A healthy option to repressing, ignoring or otherwise stuffing emotions starts with me giving myself permission to experience all emotions. I give myself permission to feel angry. I give myself permission to feel frustrated. I give myself permission to feel incompetent, or anxious, or happy, or joyful. For me: I give myself permission to feel happy on this cruise unconditionally. I recognize that feelings are not right or wrong, good or bad. They simply are. It's about me recognizing that those depending on me will be better served by the healthiest version of me.

The process of reflecting on our emotions gives us insight into our underlying motives and desires, and that insight can help us understand how to have our needs met in ways that are acceptable and adaptable.

After I name the emotion, I am wise to reflect on why I experienced *that* particular emotion in response to the stimulus. Why did I feel angry (versus sad or afraid or relieved or confused) by that parent's response? The process of reflecting on our emotions gives us insight into our underlying motives and desires, and that insight can help us understand how to have our needs met in ways that are acceptable and adaptable.

Expressing Emotions

Once we've given ourselves permission to experience all emotions, we've positioned ourselves to engage the second aspect of emotional wellbeing, which is to appropriately express emotion. I want to key in on that word: *appropriately*.

Let's get back to that potentially challenging emotion of anger. Say I'm the guy that walks around the campus with a perpetual frown on my face. Everyone knows that I am Adam, the campus grump—whatever the issue, I will be able to frame it negatively and understand it in the worst possible light. That raise we got this year? Please. It just means that much more I'm going to have to pay in taxes. Let's also say that you, being the kind, compassionate human being that you are, recognize that I am miserable, and as an act of kindness, you see me in the teacher's lounge and you decide that you want to reach out to me, the campus grump, in the hope of building some kind of supportive collegial friendship. You are brave like that.

"How are you doing today, Adam?" you ask me. Your affect is bright and cheerful, and you're hoping your smile will cause me to lower my guard. It doesn't.

"How am *I* doing today?" I respond, with loud, pressured speech. "I'll tell you how I'm doing. I'm miserable."

"Oh," you answer, immediately sorry you asked. You're ready to end the interaction. It was a mistake, you realize, to have thought that your kindness was any kind of match for my bitterness. "Well, have a good day," you say, making a beeline for the exit. But as you turn to walk away, you realize I'm not done.

"Okay, fine. I'll tell you why I'm miserable if you really want to know," I continue. You don't really want to know, which is why you didn't ask for details and turned for the door. But it's too late.

"I'm miserable because I have to work on this campus. Most of you are complete idiots. The administration on this campus and in this district is incompetent. The kids on this campus are disrespectful snots. And their parents don't care. I'm overworked, underpaid, and underappreciated. I'm thinking about leaving this hell hole because it's obvious that you all don't appreciate what you have in me."

You know I'm really not going to leave because I've been threatening that for the last sixteen years. I turn around and walk out. You take a deep sigh and slowly head for the door, your stomach half turned in knots from the negative energy I just released.

Guess what? I go home that night, and I sleep like a baby. Absolutely no problems initiating and sustaining sleep with me. Why? Because there is no emotional fuel stored in my body—I vomited it all on you in the teacher's lounge. And while that may be good for me in the short-term, consider the damage I've done in the process of expressing my anger. I've slandered my colleagues, belittled the students and their parents.

Not good. Not adaptive.

My point here is that to be healthy emotionally, we must move beyond simply expressing our emotions, keeping in

To be healthy emotionally, we must move beyond simply expressing our emotions, keeping in mind . . . how we choose to express them.

mind that *how* we choose to express them—our word choice, our nonverbal communication, and our paraverbal communication—all have the potential to express something well beyond simply how we feel about a given situation.

Our goal is to be responsible. If I do not express my emotions responsibly with my colleagues, I lose credibility and isolate myself from relational connections that were meant to be a valuable professional resource to me. I lose the privilege not only to find support as I share my professional struggles, but also to share the joys and victories along the way. Similarly, if I do not express my emotions responsibly in my interaction with my students, I lose credibility and respect. When student behavior evokes emotions in me that render me accusatory, blaming, demeaning, and unsympathetic, how can I expect my students to take me seriously when I ask them to be mature in how they manage their emotions? Same deal with parents: when I give myself permission to use intense emotion to lash out or shame parents, I surrender my authority, my platform, and the respect I receive from parents.

Meet Ms. Dunn

I crowned Ms. Dunn the queen of directing emotion after that Thursday morning I observed Tony in her classroom many years ago, my first year practicing as a school psychologist. I had never before seen anything like what happened in her classroom that day, and it was a lesson that lives with me to this day. Let me tell you the story, and then I'll dissect it to illustrate the subtext and what it has to do with directing emotion.

Ms. Dunn taught an adaptive behavior class—a self-contained class for students who had been diagnosed with an emotional disturbance. The class consisted of eight middle-school boys, all of them much bigger than Ms. Dunn. Her class was simple in its decoration—a few posters on the walls with common motivational slogans, a bean-bag in a corner as a "reflection area." Ms. Dunn requested consultation with me to develop intervention strategies to increase her effectiveness with Tony.

Tony. Everyone knew Tony. That huge file my special education director gave me my first week on the job? It was Tony's. Whatever student risk factors have been identified over the course of the last twenty years of research, Tony seemed to have them all. *That* was Tony.

I walked into Ms. Dunn's classroom at 8:48 a.m., and quietly sat in the back of her class. I pulled out my laptop and, for the first fifteen minutes, kept my eyes down, focused on the computer. Tony was so quiet and compliant, it almost made me wonder why Ms. Dunn had requested my consultation.

Then it started. At 9:03 a.m. there were signs of restlessness—pencil tapping, shifting in the desk, bouncing knee, deep sighs. "An increase in psychomotor agitation" is how we would refer to it in psychobabble.

"Tony, I'm wondering if you're feeling okay," Ms. Dunn noted to Tony in a warm, supportive tone. She approached him at his desk. "I see that your knee is bouncing a lot, and you've taken several deep sighs. Is there anything I can do to help you?" she added, almost in a whisper.

Tony said nothing. Ms. Dunn stepped back a few feet. Tony was quiet and still for about thirty seconds. Then, it started again—more pencil tapping (only louder), more shifting (this time standing up from his desk), and more deep sighs. He was clearly agitated.

"Tony, I'm pretty sure something is bothering you." Ms. Dunn's tone changed. She hadn't raised the volume of her voice, but her tone was firm this time. "The expectation, Tony, is that you will remain seated and do your work. Please sit down now."

Tony did not sit down. In fact, what happened next was something of a blur. Tony shouted a few key profanities, grabbed his textbook, and threw it across the room. Then, he stared at Ms. Dunn as if to communicate *"Ball is in your court now. Lady. Whatcha got?"*

Ms. Dunn did or said absolutely nothing for a full fifteen seconds. It felt like a day. Finally, she responded.

"Tony, we reviewed the class rules at the beginning of the year." Her tone was still firm, but at no point did she raise her voice. "We agreed that physical and verbal aggression will not be tolerated. You've broken the rule, and you will receive a consequence. But I want you to know something. When you threw that book, you deliberately threw it down at the floor. I remember at the very beginning of the year, when you threw things, you would try to hit people. You are learning to be safer. You are moving in the right direction. I'm proud of you for that progress."

Then, Ms. Dunn broke visual and verbal interaction with Tony, turned around, and returned to her desk. That was it—by 9:20, the show was over. Well, at least that act of it, anyway.

What happened with Tony that morning may seem fairly commonplace to you. Maybe it was the kind of thing that happens multiple times per hour in your classroom. Although Tony's behaviors that morning might be commonplace to you, I can almost guarantee that Ms. Dunn's responses to Tony throughout that episode certainly were not commonplace. Let me break it down to illustrate all that went on during that observation period, and how it could have gone so much worse.

> *Tony was so quiet and compliant, it almost made me wonder why Ms. Dunn had requested my consultation.*

Of course he was. It's called the Hawthorne effect. In the 1950s, researcher Henry Landsberger was curious about how changes in the work environment would impact employee performance. He asked Hawthorne Works, and electric company, if he could examine the relationship between changing light and brightness levels in the factory and worker productivity. One interpretation of the results suggested that it wasn't so much the changing light levels that impacted the workers' productivity, but the fact that the workers knew they were being observed. If I had left the observation period after only ten minutes and assumed that Tony was fine, I would have been missing the point; it's not so much whether a student can hold it together when a stranger walks in the classroom, but how long before they can no longer suppress physical and verbal aggression that is a real measure of the student's coping capacity. Tony held it together for fifteen minutes—that was a pretty good run for Tony.

At 9:03 a.m. there were signs of restlessness—pencil tapping, shifting in the desk, bouncing knee, deep sighs ... "Tony, I'm wondering if you're feeling okay," Ms. Dunn noted to Tony in a warm, supportive tone. She approached him at his desk. "I see that your knee is bouncing a lot, and you've taken several deep sighs. Is there anything I can do to help you?" she added, almost in a whisper.

Already, things could have gone wrong here. What if Ms. Dunn had simply approached Tony and said, "Tony, please stop making so much noise. You're distracting everyone"? Or, maybe insulting sarcasm: "Tony, I see you obviously forgot to take your meds today." Tony probably would have perceived such responses as a threat or insult and escalated more quickly. At that point, Ms. Dunn might have had challenging thoughts: *I don't get paid enough to put up with this. Why did I get stuck with Tony? Why won't he just do what I tell him to do?* In addition to those challenging thoughts, she also may have experienced challenging feelings: she may have felt frustrated at the possibility of having to start with Tony this early in the morning. She also might have felt threatened by the possibility that Tony was going to make her look incompetent with me, "the expert," observing.

I'm not sure what Ms. Dunn was thinking or feeling in that moment, but her response was perfect. Instead of taking the approach I just described, Ms. Dunn saw Tony escalating, and her first response was to offer support. In essence, "How can I help you?" In that step, she also modeled emotional awareness for Tony, linking his feelings with a behavior. The hope would be that Tony would eventually develop an internal awareness of how to recognize his own emotion based on what his body was telling him.

Tony was quiet and still for about thirty seconds. Then, it started again—more pencil tapping (only louder), more shifting (this time standing up from his desk), and more deep sighs). He was clearly agitated. "Tony, I'm pretty sure something is bothering you." Ms. Dunn's tone changed. She hadn't raised the volume of her voice, but her tone was firm this time. "The expectation, Tony, is that you will remain seated and do your work. Please sit down now."

Here, we have yet another fork in the road. One option: "Tony, how many times do I have to tell you not to make noise. You're still bothering everyone. You just don't get it, do you? Now you better cut it out right now. Do you want me to send you to the office? And it's only 9:00 in the morning. God, help me. It's gonna be a long day, isn't it?" At that point, Ms. Dunn's thoughts and feelings, like Tony's, might have been escalating as well. *"I can't stand this kid. I know he's got it in for me. Dr. Sáenz probably thinks I am a completely ineffective idiot at this point, and he's probably going to tell my principal that he's pretty sure I shouldn't even be a teacher."* These thoughts probably would be accompanied by increased feelings of frustration, fear, and anxiety.

Again, I don't know what her thoughts or feelings were at that point, but Ms. Dunn responded perfectly. She realized that her initial attempts to help Tony de-escalate by supporting him were not successful, and she knew it was time to be directive. She didn't raise the volume of her voice, but she shifted her tone distinctly enough that Tony knew her position changed. She pointed out the rule that Tony was breaking, and directed him to be compliant. As you recall, Tony was not compliant. He was, in fact, everything but compliant.

Ms. Dunn did or said absolutely nothing for a full fifteen seconds. It felt like a day. Finally, she responded. "Tony, we reviewed the class rules at the beginning of the year." Her tone was still firm, but at no point did she raise her voice. "We agreed that physical and verbal aggression will not be tolerated. You've broken the rule, and you will receive a consequence. But I want you to know something. When you threw that book, you deliberately threw it down at the floor.

I remember at the very beginning of the year, when you threw things, you would try to hit people. You are learning to be safer. You are moving in the right direction. I'm proud of you for that progress."

Here, we have what I believe was the height of Ms. Dunn's demonstrated brilliance. The last fork in the road, option one: "That's it, Tony! I've had it with you! Get out of my class right now, and if you don't get out right now, I'll call the resource officer and have him remove you! How would you like *that*?"

I'm sure you can easily imagine the thoughts and feelings that Ms. Dunn might have experienced at that moment. I don't know what they were, but I'm sure they were intense: that's why she paused for fifteen seconds. In that highly charged moment, with Tony baiting her, Ms. Dunn knew she was losing control, and she knew that maintaining control of herself was the first priority. She was wise. She stopped, taking a fifteen-second self-imposed time out to collect herself. Not only did that pause afford her an opportunity to collect herself, but it also broke the rhythm of the escalating pattern of interaction she and Tony were experiencing. Further still, as she focused on regulating herself, she was modeling for Tony what effective anger management looked like. She was admitting to him that she was a fallible human being, capable—like him—of becoming angry and frustrated when things didn't go her way. Then, after she collected herself, she immediately described the rule Tony broke and gave him a consequence. She didn't let his aggressive behavior intimidate her out of enforcing rules.

But here was the kicker for me: *she praised him*. After all that, with Tony demanding so much from her and pushing her to that point of emotional intensity, she managed to find something—anything—positive in his performance to encourage and reinforce his progress. Ms. Dunn was brilliant like that. She seemed to always be able to engage admittedly challenging, relationship-eroding situations and turn them into relationship-building situations. She didn't allow her thoughts to bring her to a point of justifying the use of her intense emotion as a fuel to attack, demean or be otherwise punishing and hurtful to Tony.

Do you see now why I crowned Ms. Dunn the queen of directing emotion? Over the years I knew and worked with Ms. Dunn, I learned that her interaction with Tony that day wasn't simply Hawthorne effect; she engaged with students, faculty, and parents with that level of awareness every day, regardless of whether I was observing her.

The payback for the individual who has made the investment in self-awareness is having an ever-increasing capacity to turn potentially relationship-eroding interactions into relationship-building interactions.

"What's the point?" some might argue. "Tony still went off on her, so what good did it do her?" My response is that our motive for regulating ourselves should not be to change anyone's behavior but our own. The payback for the individual who has made the investment in self-awareness is having an ever-increasing capacity to turn potentially relationship-eroding interactions into relationship-building interactions. If I value becoming and being that kind of human being, then I will work to that end regardless of whether others around me change.

Think about how many potentially challenging interactions you may have—verbal, nonverbal, email, text messages, and otherwise—with students, parents or colleagues each day. Wouldn't you love to know that you have optimized yourself to turn those potentially problematic interactions into opportunities to build greater relational connection? That level of emotional self-awareness and self-regulation is a skill, like shooting a basketball or running a marathon; its development is neither natural nor effort-free.

The Environment/Feeling/Thought Connection

We know, then, that on the one hand, while emotional self-awareness and modulation require effort on our part, the benefits are great. On the other hand, when we are not practicing and developing our emotional intelligence, the results are corrosive to relationships and render us isolated and discredited.

How do we develop this skill? There are many approaches, to be sure, but I'm going to focus on an approach we use in cognitive therapy. In essence, cognitive therapy is a form of treatment that focuses on the relationships among thoughts, feelings, and behaviors; since the three are inter-connected, there is a two-way cause-and-effect relationship among them.

The idea is to focus on thoughts and change thoughts to ease distressful feelings. The interaction starts with a stimulus, either external (e.g., a student escalates, a parent sends a nasty email, or a colleague criticizes our work in a staff meeting) or internal (e.g., I feel sad today or I can't stop thinking about my next performance evaluation). Whether the trigger is internal or external, the typical pattern is to engage in a feedback loop that may not, in the end, make our lives better. Changing our thoughts can change our feelings, and easing distressful feelings can keep us from engaging automatic (and often non-productive) responses. When we are not dealing with the interference of distressful feelings, we are more able to engage thoughtful and deliberate—often called "mindful"—responses. The list below illustrates how the pattern can play out.

1. *The trigger*: I received an email from a parent with the words "Please Call My Lawyer" in the subject line.

2. *The feeling(s)*: Fear, defensiveness, mild curiosity.

3. *The thought(s)*: I'm going to lose my job. If I lose my job, I won't be able to pay my bills. My family and I will end up homeless. I have finally been exposed as a fraud and failure.

4. *The automatic response*: I do or say anything possible to placate this parent, OR I avoid this situation, delete the email and pretend I never read it, OR I attack first by hiring a lawyer of my own and sue the family for my pain and suffering.

Doesn't this scenario just seem miserable? Of course it is. Who would want to open their email and find this? We would be very justified in feeling fear, anxiety, and defensiveness—no problem there. The question, though, is whether the automatic response at the end of that series makes our life better or worse. In the example noted above, the thoughts listed are a form of catastrophizing, which is the habit of assuming the worst-case and often irrational end to a given scenario. Consider an alternate response to the same trigger:

1. *The trigger*: I received an email from a parent with the words "Please Call My Lawyer" in the subject line.
2. *The feeling(s)*: Fear, defensiveness, mild curiosity.
3. *The NEW thought(s)*: This is not fun. But it's only an email. I don't know what this is about.
4. *The MINDFUL response*: I should forward this email to my administrator and get some feedback before I respond to the parent.

Notice that the trigger and feelings are still the same. What is different, though, are the thoughts I choose to attend to following the trigger and the feelings. Here is another example of the pattern as it relates to the scenario with Ms. Dunn. First, I have outlined how the pattern may have played out negatively:

1. *The trigger*: Tony is agitated and not doing what I have asked him to.
2. *The feeling(s)*: Frustrated, angry, impatient.
3. *The thought(s)*: No one in this room respects me.
4. *The automatic response*: Say something to shock Tony into compliance or into a complete meltdown so I can have him removed from my class.

1. *The trigger*: Tony is agitated and not doing what I have asked him to.
2. *The feeling(s)*: Frustrated, angry, impatient.
3. *The NEW thought(s)*: It's okay for me to feel frustrated, angry, and impatient. I also know I can't let what I feel become a fuel to drive me to an inappropriate or unhelpful response to Tony.

4. *The MINDFUL response*: I will first offer Tony support. If that doesn't help him, I will be directive with Tony. If that doesn't help him, I will administer a consequence. I will maintain my dignity and Tony's throughout the process.

Now, I'd like you to take some time to reflect on situations with your students, with parents, and with colleagues. Which moments trigger you the most? An insult to your job performance? An insult to some physical attribute about which you are quietly and deeply insecure? Apathy? After you've identified your triggers, identify the feelings those triggers evoke. Then, write down the thoughts you might have in the context of that trigger and those feelings. Be honest. Finally, write your automatic response: what do you typically do instinctively when you are faced with that trigger that evokes those feelings and those thoughts? Again, be honest.

If your automatic responses to your triggers are adaptive (meaning they are appropriate and facilitate an effective, healthy resolution to the trigger), good for you. That means that you know your triggers, and that you are self-aware enough that the emotions that spike in you after the triggering event do not have an inappropriate control over you. If, though, your automatic responses are maladaptive (meaning they have the potential to inflict relational damage), you are wise to re-examine your thoughts and create new thought patterns that will de-escalate your emotional state. Thoughts like "These kids have absolutely no respect" can become "I will maintain my self-respect and dignity regardless of how I perceive that I am treated by others." Thoughts like "I am so sick of disengaged parents" can become "I choose to do my best work regardless of parental involvement." Thoughts like "The faculty on this campus are toxic and back-biting" can become "I will model appropriate, mature, and loving interactions with all my colleagues, regardless of how they choose to relate with me or anyone else."

With Students

1. *The trigger*:
2. *The feeling(s)*:
3. *The thought(s)*:
4. *The automatic response*:

1. *The trigger*:
2. *The feeling(s)*:
3. *The NEW thought(s)*:
4. *The MINDFUL response*:

With Colleagues

1. *The trigger*:
2. *The feeling(s)*:
3. *The thought(s)*:
4. *The automatic response*:

1. *The trigger*:
2. *The feeling(s)*:
3. *The NEW thought(s)*:
4. *The MINDFUL response*:

With Parents

1. *The trigger*:
2. *The feeling(s)*:
3. *The thought(s)*:
4. *The automatic response*:

1. *The trigger*:
2. *The feeling(s)*:
3. *The NEW thought(s)*:
4. *The MINDFUL response*:

How Directing Impacts Relationships

Each day presents us with literally hundreds of trigger moments. Can I find what I need to be ready for work? Are the kids ready? How is traffic? What will my administrator say about the project I'm working on? When will the "Tony" in my class go off today? On and on we could go, with each scenario creating a unique emotion-evoking experience; each scenario adds into my tank the fuel of emotion, which, if not directed appropriately, can be an explosive force externally or a corrosive force internally.

The good news is that as I increase my skill in appropriately directing my emotion (by changing and focusing on different thoughts about the experience), trigger moments lose their destructive power. In fact, trigger moments actually have the potential to become opportunities to develop deeper, more authentic relational connection.

> *As I increase my skill in appropriately directing my emotion (by changing and focusing on different thoughts about the experience), trigger moments lose their destructive power.*

Key Point Summary

♦ Emotion is energy.

♦ To experience an emotion is simply to acknowledge its presence. Chronic denying, stuffing or minimizing emotions is highly correlated with negative physical and psychological outcomes.

♦ Emotion can be expressed physically or verbally, and either option has the potential to be helpful or hurtful.

♦ Changing the thoughts we have about triggers and the resulting feelings is an effective method to reduce the negative impact triggering events and uncomfortable emotions can have on us.

"*Sometimes, reaching out and taking someone's hand is the beginning of a journey. At other times, it is allowing another to take yours.*"
Vera Nazarian, *The Perpetual Calendar of Inspiration*

"*The important element is the way in which all things are connected. Every thought and action sends shivers of energy into the world around us, which affects all creation. Perceiving the world as a web of connectedness helps us to overcome the feelings of separation that hold us back and cloud our vision. This connection with all life increases our sense of responsibility for every move, every attitude, allowing us to see clearly that each soul does indeed make a difference to the whole.*"
Emma Restall Orr, *Druidry*

4

Connecting
Can I Build a Bridge?

Philosophers Immanuel Kant and John Stuart Mill argued for the value of individual autonomy, an idea that is generally understood to refer to the capacity to be one's own person and to live one's life according to self-embraced values (versus values that have been forged or coerced by external institutional forces). In psychology, we use the term "individuation" to capture this idea. Individuation is about the adult individual consciously evaluating the traditions, values, customs, and expectations that were modeled by the individual's family of origin, and then mindfully choosing which to embrace or discard. Individuation can be difficult because the individual may risk rejection by the family if the individual chooses to no longer embrace certain aspects of the family's ethic. Thus, individuation is about autonomy and the capacity to be one's authentic self. This is the adult saying, "I grew up Christian, but I'm not sure I believe in God," or "When I was a child, my mother confided in me about inappropriate intimate details of her marital problems with my father; I will make sure I allow my children to be my children and not turn them into my personal confidants."

I have grown to value, both personally and professionally, the process of individuation and the resulting autonomy. I give three cheers.

The reason I raise the point, though, is to note that while I value personal responsibility and autonomy, I also have concerns about what I perceive to be, at its worst, an over-emphasis on what former U.S. president Herbert Hoover referred to as rugged individualism. Of course, in the context of Hoover's speech, rugged individualism referred to the individual's ability to survive by helping him- or herself, without government assistance. The rugged individualism that concerns me is not so much a politic about government involvement in the affairs of the individual as it is the broader idea of the individual's separateness from his or her fellow human beings; I worry when individualism becomes isolationism.

Consider the words of English poet John Donne:

> No man is an island entire of itself; every man is a piece of the continent, a part of the main. If a clod be washed away by the sea, Europe is the less, as well as if a promontory were, as well as if a manor of thy friend's or of thine own were. Any man's death diminishes me, because I am involved in mankind. And therefore never send to know for whom the bell tolls: it tolls for thee.

What Donne is communicating here, in beautiful poetry, is the idea I addressed earlier with my Lego analogy: because we were created for one another, we need each other. Because we need each other, then, our goal should be to find healthy, adaptive interdependence; interdependence is that sometimes seemingly evasive middle ground that lies between the extremes of isolating independence and enmeshed co-dependence.

Our goal should be to find healthy, adaptive interdependence; interdependence is that sometimes seemingly evasive middle ground that lies between the extremes of isolating independence and enmeshed co-dependence.

How do we find that middle ground? We connect. We build bridges—relational pathways that allow us to come when we need to come and leave when we need to leave.

About Good Bridge Builders

Thank God for good bridge builders. This is the person that perceives the slightest downward change in your countenance and asks if everything is okay. This is the person that remembers on Monday that last weekend was your big event and goes out of her way to ask you how it went. If you are an educator, you are probably a good bridge builder. My experience tells me that most educators are nurturers, since at its core, educating is about fostering growth.

But what about this: what if you are an educator who loves your content area, but who is perceived by students, parents or colleagues as unapproachable? What if you are the kind of educator that values completing tasks above and at the expense of relationships? What if you are an educator who is absolutely drained by being around other people?

Maybe I just activated your defenses. "Connection is not necessary because I'm an introvert," you say. Or this: "Connection may be necessary, but I'm not about to put myself out there again after the way I've been hurt by these students or parents or colleagues." If some part of you is resisting the idea that we—that *you* in particular—need to be connected, I think this chapter may be particularly relevant for you. Even in the absence of past pain that keeps us from reaching out again, even when we have a clean bill of emotional health, there is a common reason we fail to connect with others.

Differences and the Protective Mechanism They Evoke

We are biologically evolved and behaviorally conditioned to perceive variance as a dashboard light. It helps keep us safe, but it takes energy. Let me explain.

Buried deep in our subconscious is something of an embedded computer program, a survival mechanism, called the fight or flight response. This program is embedded so deep in our subconscious that it can activate and move our body to action without our even realizing it. Here's a simple example: think about the last time you were burned, maybe by an oven. Did you really have to stop to process whether the stove was hot? And whether it was so hot that it presented danger? And whether, then, you should move your hand? And if so, where should you move it to? Of course you didn't. In that example, your fight or flight program did an over-ride of your conscious thought process and activated your body into some action that protected you, either by attacking the source of the stress or by withdrawing from it (in this case, withdrawal).

That same fight or flight response mechanism impacts our ability to connect with others because it is activated at varying levels of our awareness when our brain perceives difference in others. This car/machine/thing is different from the car/machine/thing I'm used to. Is it safe? This neighborhood/people group/value system is different from my neighborhood/people group/value system. Is it safe?

The process of filtering through differences to assess safety can be exhausting, and that is, generally speaking, why most of us experience change as a stressful phenomenon. Change has the potential to bring entire arenas of difference, and through all that resulting difference, we must sort and process to assess safety. And since change and the resulting differences we must process can exhaust us, most of us find rhythms and patterns—in a word, predictability—to decrease the energy output necessary to process difference. Usually, we end up spending the most time with people who look like us, sound like us, believe what we believe, and value what we value.

There are essential benefits to living that way, such as a sense of shared community and purpose. This is good. However, self-induced homogeneity can have its down sides, and in my mind, the implications can be significant. My biologically-programmed need for sameness can mean that my interaction with people with different ethnic identities, cultural identities, socioeconomic identities, gender identities, or religious identities can be contaminated (*at levels of which I am not even aware*) by a self-protective barrier. In other words, something deep within me *automatically* responds to those who are different from me either by creating distance (often, in the form of avoiding) or attacking (often, in the form of judging).

I was searching for a way to better understand and communicate the relationship between the activation of the fight or flight mechanism and our ability to connect with others, so I emailed my colleague, Dr. James Deegear, a staff psychologist at the Texas A&M Student Counseling Service. James understands this concept at a personal level. For ten years, his wife, Kellie—a Caucasian female who grew up in an upper middle-class family—was principal at an elementary school (a) whose predominant ethnic demographic was Hispanic and African American and (b) which was located in an economically disadvantaged neighborhood. There were many differences for Kellie and her faculty to overcome. James and Kellie began to explore exactly how those differences were limiting the faculty's success in building relationships with students.

Through our series of email exchanges, James summarized it beautifully. He gave me permission to share his response.

From: James Deegear <xxxxxxx@gmail.com>   Mon, Dec 22,
                                            2014 at 12:04 PM
To: Adam Saenz <adam@adamsaenz.com>

Adam,
     Because we have a biological 'need' to see difference, we make categorical assumptions as a protective/self-preservation development. Our responsibility is to suspend those tendencies and see people beyond differences. If our tendency is to judge based on differences, our challenge is to suspend judgment by recognizing and emphasizing our similarities with others (which are often less visible). What struggles do these kids [or their parents or my colleagues] have that are in some way similar to my own struggles? What shared experience do we have? When we can do this, then, we have a place for empathy (versus a judging sympathy) for others.

As I contemplated James' email responses and reflected back to conversations I have been fortunate to have had with James and Kellie, the concept of empathy emerged as a key material necessary to build bridges to connect with others.

Let's explore empathy.

Do You Feel Like We Do
(and See Like We Do)?

Theresa Wiseman is a nurse trainer at the Bloomsbury and Islington College of Nursing in England. She was curious about the role empathy played in the nurse's delivery of health care, so she conducted a meta-analysis of thirty-three studies on empathy. Among her key findings was the idea that the presence of empathy functions as both a state and a trait. What that means is that a certain level of empathy is statically present in everyone; it's a trait, like eye color. The degree to which the individual expresses empathy, though, can vary across situations. In that regard, then, empathy is a dynamic state, like an emotion or the weather. The implication is that only the deeply impaired, diagnosable sociopath can say, "Sorry. I'm just not an empathetic individual." The real question is not whether we have empathy, but to what degree we *choose* to express it. Thus, the expression of empathy is a skill, and just as I must practice to play a musical instrument well, I also must practice if I want to demonstrate empathy well.

Wiseman's second key finding was that all studies pointed to common traits of empathy, which can be summarized as follows: Effective empathy is seeing and feeling what the other sees and feels, accepting without judgment what the other sees and feels, and then reflecting back to the other what they see or feel. Empathy says, "I want to overcome my own resistance that I might know your situation as you know your situation." Empathy is worlds apart from sympathy, which is simply feeling sorry for someone else who is suffering. The power of empathy underscores the notion that more deeply, or perhaps more importantly, than wanting fixes to our problems, we need to know that we are not alone in our suffering.

Effective empathy is seeing and feeling what the other sees and feels, accepting without judgment what the other sees and feels, and then reflecting back to the other what they see or feel.

What would empathy look like for the educator? Something like this, I think:

You, student, who are a hot mess, with your drug problem, your behavior problem, your academic problem, your social problem, your apathy problem. You who are different from me in so many ways and on so many levels. Yes, you. I choose to get past my intense desire to either avoid you or judge you for the inconvenience you present in my life. I purpose to focus on seeing what you see, feeling what you feel, and then I will reflect back to you that I know what you see and feel.

You, parent, who engage only to blame, with your disrespectful demeanor and threats to call my superintendent and your lawyer. You and I are different in so many ways and on so many levels. Yes, you. I choose to get past my intense desire to either avoid you or judge you for the inconvenience you present in my life. I purpose to focus on seeing what you see, feeling what you feel, and then reflecting back to you that I know what you see and feel.

You, colleague, who are toxic and bitter, with your negative word for every employee and student on this campus and your utter inability to take responsibility for your role. You who are different from me in so many ways and on so many levels. Yes, you. I choose to get past my intense desire to either avoid you or judge you for the inconvenience you present in my life. I purpose to focus on seeing what you see, feeling what you feel, and then I will reflect back to you that I know what you see and feel.

This is no small task. I really do get that. Empathy requires something from us, something deep, and I don't know that we ever will grow fluid in our capacity to deliver it until we begin to understand empathy's power to connect us. Before I tell you about Coach Rivera—the absolute Michael Jordan of empathy in my book—I want to touch on the role of non-contingent communication (to me, empathy's first cousin) in bridge-building.

Looking Past the Thing About You That Bothers Me

To understand non-contingent communication, we must first understand contingent communication. For our purpose, contingent communication is communication that is dependent on or initiated by the other's behavior: *"John, please sit down."* *"Adam, what are you supposed to be doing right now?"* Often, a great deal of communication that happens in the classroom is contingent communication. What tends to happen when teacher communication is dependent on student behavior is that the behavior that evokes communication will be inappropriate behavior. In other words, if I only verbally engage my students based on their behavior, it will probably end up being negative student behavior that will cause me to initiate communication, as in the examples I just mentioned. The message students get, then, is that if they want your attention, they will have to misbehave to get it.

Contrast that to non-contingent communication. As you probably guessed, non-contingent communication is not dependent on or triggered by student behavior. It can be a question or a comment: *"How was your weekend?"* *"If you were a famous musician or a famous athlete, what would you say to all the parents out there?"* *"I love that shirt."* *"I saw a great movie/game last weekend."* Even a simple observation can work: *"I see you're wearing your red shirt today."* I can offer these invitations regardless of what a student is or is not doing.

Here's how I learned the value of non-contingent communication. Early in my career as a school psychologist, I often was called to campuses to de-escalate highly charged situations with students who were having meltdowns. Invariably, I would enter the building, follow my ears, and arrive to a scene with five or six adults hovering around an obviously aroused child. Looking back, I think there was an unspoken expectation that I, the licensed psychologist, would show up, wave my magic Ph.D. wand, and make everything better. That's what I expected, anyway.

I figured out pretty quickly that "Hello, Escalated Student. My name is Dr. Adam Sáenz, and I'm here to help you" didn't impress Escalated Student. In fact, Escalated Student didn't care where I had earned my doctorate or where I had keynoted the week before. He didn't care about what I had to say or any recommendations I had to offer in the heat of the moment. I also figured out pretty quickly not to take it personally; Escalated Student was equally as unimpressed with the officer who had a badge and a side-arm.

But time after time, do you know whom a kid like Escalated Student *would* respond to? It wasn't necessarily the person with the most authority, or the most degrees, or the most muscle. It was the adult on campus with whom he had experienced the most non-contingent communication. Those were the adults that knew Escalated Student and had a relationship with him. Sometimes that person was the principal or the behavior management specialist, but sometimes it was the custodian or the paraprofessional or the diminutive woman who served his lunch. The bottom line was that only the individuals who had made the investment to get to know Escalated Student by interacting with him in a non-contingent manner could reap the dividend of being able to speak into his life when he was highly charged or escalated; because they had made such deep investments in his relational account, he afforded them the privilege to make withdrawals on rainy days.

I'm using a student-based experience to illustrate the value of non-contingent communication. Rest assured, though, that non-contingent communication is an effective strategy to build a bridge with a colleague, a parent—anyone. If you want to know more about non-contingent communication, visit this website: www.conversationstarters.com.

Meet Coach Williams

I'm not sure I know anyone more skilled in combining empathy and non-contingent communication than Coach Williams. Here's what I learned from him as he connected with a mom I'll just call Ms. Martinez. I never saw it coming—this Caucasian male building trust and rapport with a mistrustful and angry first generation Latina.

Ms. Martinez's son, Nicodemus, was a challenge, not just to his teacher, not just to the sixth grade, but to the entire campus. He had attended four different elementary schools in the district since second grade, making it particularly difficult for any particular campus faculty to really build a relationship with him. I had consulted with each of the four campuses every time he moved.

The deal with Nicodemus, though, was that in his not-so-intense moments, he could be incredibly charming, and endearing. That went a long way to allowing us to stay connected to our hope for him and to our belief that his core was good and sweet, and that some day, that good, sweet core would emerge and dominate.

Ms. Martinez, however, was a different story. I had no hope for her. I saw no good, sweet core. Whatever hope or goodness I talked myself into on her behalf was destroyed that morning she delivered to the principal a profanity-laced tirade at the school entry in front of children, parents and staff alike (because her son's teacher "was out to get him"). She had never been quite that verbally aggressive toward me, but she would regularly lodge her verbal fiery arrows my way as I attempted to include her in my individual work with her son; it was not uncommon for her to blame me for his failure or tell me that I obviously had no clue what I was doing with him.

I won't say I hated Ms. Martinez. I really didn't. What I felt when I had to interact with her (or when I even thought of her) was somewhere between condescension and, if I'm totally honest, deep judgment of her as a fundamentally inferior human being. Question: Why did her son show up to school every day wearing dirty and tattered clothes, and she drove a car that was more expensive than mine? My answer: because she was a fundamentally inferior human being. Question: Why did she move four times to live with four different paramours when I knew through individual counseling with her son that he desperately needed attention and stability? My answer: because she was a fundamentally inferior human being.

I didn't realize it at a heart level at the time, but this belief I held about Ms. Martinez's inherent worth crippled my ability to connect with her. Inevitably, I walked into and away from every interaction with her mentally on-guard, just waiting for her to speak the wrong thing, look the wrong way, answer the wrong way—anything that would confirm that I was correct in my judgment of her and justified in my writing her off. She must have sensed that in me. In many ways, I was creating a self-fulfilling prophecy.

It wasn't just me. I think I can say with accuracy that no one on that campus liked her. No one wanted to interact with her or be around her. We as a staff had become so skewed that we quit trying to pretend that we didn't like her. We gave ourselves permission to roll our eyes, sigh deeply, or make a sarcastic remark whenever her name came up. It was not the best moment for me nor for the faculty on that campus.

Except for Coach Williams. He never caved in to that group-think: I never heard him speak ill of Ms. Martinez, or roll his eyes or sigh deeply at the mention of her name. In fact, he often went out of his way to say good morning and visit with her when she dropped her son off. Sometimes their visits would last several minutes. It always struck me as odd—this burly, Caucasian man going out of his way to interact with this seemingly toxic Latina, Mexican American woman. What did they have to talk about? Why did he make a point to connect with her?

One day, after the students had filed in and first period had started, I saw Coach Williams walking toward me in the hallway. I just came out and asked him.

"Good morning, Coach," I said as I approached him. "Listen, I've got a random question for you I hope you don't mind me asking. I think it's safe for me to say that no one really likes being around Ms. Martinez—you know Nicodemus' mom—but you seem to go out of your way to interact with her and be nice to her. What is the deal? Do you know her personally, or outside school?"

I could tell by his expression on his face that he wasn't expecting the question. He paused for a moment.

"No, I don't really know her outside school," he finally said.

"So, what do you two talk about? It seems like every time I interact with her it's about her son, and what's not working, and what I need her to do to help us reach him," I continued. "And it seems like she always just responds with some kind of nasty comment."

"Yeah," he said with a small chuckle. "She's ripped into me a few times, too. I try not to focus on that, though. Honestly, Adam, I usually just ask how her morning went. If she had a problem or something didn't go right, I just listen. Sometimes

I ask if there's anything I can do to help Nicodemus at school on any given day. If she doesn't seem in a hurry, I'll ask about her weekend."

"Really?" I asked. "What's the point?"

He paused again. I'll never forget his response.

"I guess the point is that she is a human being, and she's suffering," he said. "I can't begin to imagine what burden she is under. I've had my share of struggles in my life, but probably not anything near what she's going through. To be honest, I'm not so sure I'd be doing half as well as she is if I were in her shoes and faced with the same obstacles . . . well, have a great day."

Then he smiled and continued on his way.

In February of that year, the principal held a staffing to assess the effectiveness of Nicodemus' behavior plan. Much to my surprise, Ms. Martinez actually participated. What surprised me even more, though, was Ms. Martinez's request as we convened in the conference room: "Can Coach Williams be here?"

That's when it really hit me: Coach Williams had built a bridge. His payoff for all those mornings of non-judgmental empathy and non-contingent communication? An invitation. That payoff may seem small, like very little return on such a very large investment. Maybe it was; it wasn't like Nicodemus suddenly started showing up in new—or even clean—clothes. It wasn't like Ms. Martinez finally settled down and purposed to create some sense of stability for Nicodemus. Nope. It was just an invitation.

I wonder, though, if we've lost the ability to appreciate baby steps. I wonder if the policy culture that creates the admittedly much-needed sense of urgency around reaching all students comes at the cost of our capacity to walk patiently with those who are struggling. I don't know. What I do know is that Coach Williams saw what Ms. Martinez saw, and he felt what she felt. Coach Williams was involved in mankind, and he knew that Ms. Martinez's bell tolled for him.

I realized in that moment that in my effort to help her son, my ego had taken the driver's seat; because I didn't feel appreciated or respected by Ms. Martinez for all I was doing to help her son, I, in my anger and resentment, gave myself permission to judge and dismiss her in a me-versus-you mentality. I—the licensed psychologist who is supposed to be the expert in human behavior—had missed the boat. Coach Williams had unwittingly proven that connecting wasn't about having advanced degrees or positions of power. It was a magnificent gut punch, and I needed it.

Connecting and Bridge-Building: A Readiness Assessment

Now we know a bit more about how empathy and non-contingent communication are essential to connecting. How naturally does connecting and bridge-building come to you? We created this assessment (see Table 4.1) to give us just a bit more of an empirical answer. Complete this assessment, and we'll tell you how your score compares with the sample group.

1 = Definitely Not True of Me

2 = Not Usually True of Me

3 = Undecided

4 = Usually True of Me

5 = Definitely True of Me

When you have completed the assessment, add your points. The highest you can score is 150, which means you rated yourself a 5 on all 30 items. The lowest you can score is a 30, which means you rated yourself a 1 on all 30 items. When we administered this rating scale to a sample of 110 teachers across grade levels and years of experience, we found an average score of 81. The lowest score was 60, and the highest score was 110.

If you scored below 61, your relationship-building may come naturally to you, as you are likely to be very accepting and accommodating of others. You probably value being relationally connected, and you probably have a very high capacity to demonstrate empathy and to practice non-contingent communication.

If you scored between 71 and 91, your bridge-building skills probably are very comparable to your colleagues. Your capacity

Table 4.1 Connecting and Bridge-Building: A Readiness Assessment

Thought/Feeling/Behavior	1	2	3	4	5
1. I feel emotionally drained after I've been in a group of people for a while.					
2. People might think I'm quiet or withdrawn.					
3. People would describe me as being able to get things done.					
4. Students in my classroom understand that what I say goes.					
5. I find more satisfaction in accomplishing a task versus getting to know people in the process.					
6. Once I've made up my mind, it's very hard to get me to change it.					
7. My students' parents understand that if they want to interact with me, there is an established time and place to do so.					
8. I am self-sufficient and do not usually ask for help.					
9. Small talk tortures me.					
10. I value anonymity.					
11. The ideal vacation involves lots of alone time, or time with few others.					
12. I usually don't maintain more than one or two friends at a time.					
13. My hobbies are mostly solo versus group activities.					
14. When I'm stressed or overwhelmed, I just want to be alone with my thoughts.					
15. I don't really care whether my students like me. I care much more that they respect me.					
16. When I know that one of my colleagues is struggling, I quietly hope they don't come to me to ask for help.					
17. Instead of having a half-day of get-to-know-you bonding with my colleagues, I'd much rather use the half-day to catch up or get ahead on my work.					

Thought/Feeling/Behavior	1	2	3	4	5
18. I am happy regardless of what my students think of me.					
19. What my students' parents think of me is not important to me.					
20. I know exactly what I want in life, and I usually get frustrated when people become obstacles to my goals.					
21. I have been described as strong-willed and opinionated.					
22. Students know in my class, there are no favorites; all the rules apply to all the students all the time.					
23. I would describe myself as more of a thinker than a feeler.					
24. I usually feel uncomfortable around people who are excessively expressive or emotional.					
25. Even in romantic relationships, I have been described as distant or emotionally unavailable.					
26. If there is a job to be done, I'd rather just do it myself instead of doing it as a group project.					
27. It's hard for me to ask for help, even when I know I need it.					
28. I absolutely cannot tolerate clutter, disorganization or messes.					
29. I don't like change.					
30. It's much easier for me to talk about my thoughts rather than my feelings.					

to demonstrate empathy and engage in non-contingent communication probably is neither a strength nor a weakness for you.

If you scored above 100, you probably are not a natural bridge builder when compared to your colleagues. You probably tend to value completing tasks above connecting with others, and practicing empathy and non-contingent communication probably is not your strong suit.

Key Point Summary

- ♦ As we encourage personal responsibility and individuality, we must keep in mind the need for connection.

- ♦ Empathy is a skill, and like the development of any other skill, requires practice to achieve fluency.

- ♦ Empathy is the ability to suspend one's judgment of another to be able to see what the other sees and feel what the other feels, and then to be able to communicate that back to them.

- ♦ Non-contingent communication is not dependent on behavior, and it is an essential form of communication in relationship-building.

"Good fences make good neighbors."

Robert Frost, *Mending Wall*

"Daring to set boundaries is about having the courage to love ourselves, even when we risk disappointing others."

Brene Brown

"If your boundary training consists only of words, you are wasting your breath. But if you 'do' boundaries with your [students], they internalize the experiences, remember them, digest them, and make them part of how they see reality."

Henry Cloud

5

Protecting
Can I Build a Fence?

We love where we practice. Our clinic is based in a house built in the late 1950s (that's ancient by Texas standards) with beautiful hardwood floors throughout and lots of windows and natural lighting. My office is in a back room that has a fireplace and a row of windows that overlooks half an acre of land into a green belt. Our patients tell us the place feels warm and inviting—the kind of place that you'd want to go to spill your guts.

The neighborhood was once a residential area, but most of the properties and lots on our busy avenue have been converted to commercial property. The exception is the property immediately to our right, which has remained a residential rental property. Over the years, we have made friends with whomever happened to live there. Then Mean Mr. Mike and his three perpetually barking German shepherds moved in. Paradise lost.

We realized fairly quickly that trying to guide a patient through progressive relaxation and biofeedback exercises is next to impossible with three dogs right outside your office wall raging like screaming banshees. Things got so bad, we were forced to go over to and visit with Mr. Mike (he hadn't yet earned the title of Mean) to see what we could do about it. Maybe place the dogs on the side of the house opposite our office? Maybe bring the dogs in his garage area during office hours?

Mr. Mike was less than open to the discussion. In fact, he seemed deeply insulted by our suggestion that his barking and growling dogs were a nuisance, and he escalated rather quickly. His string of yelled profanities ended with "and I am going to put my #&$^% dogs right outside your window so they can terrorize your patients all day long!" *That* was when Mr. Mike earned his title.

We felt stuck. We called animal control to investigate options. We called the city zoning department to investigate options. We called the police department to investigate options. In the end, we learned that all we could do was build a barrier between our property and his. So, that's exactly what we did. We hired a survey company to come out and establish the property lines, and then we hired a contractor to build a ten-foot-high picket fence between our property and Mean Mr. Mikes.

Mean Mr. Mike was furious when he realized what we were doing. He had a team of lawyers, he said. He had guns, he said. You don't go to war with Mr. Mike, he said. As the contractors were building the fence, he raged at them so violently that we were forced to call the police. In the end, though, the fence created an effective visual barrier for and from the dogs, and kept them much less interested in that part of their property. The barking subsided. We felt safe again.

Mean Mr. Mike still lives next door. We see him from time to time, but we never exchange anything more than glances. What a valuable lesson we learned about setting boundaries.

What Is Building a Fence in Relationships?

Boundaries are about knowing what belongs to me and what does not belong to me. Establishing boundaries contributes to our sense of safety because they allow everyone to know—just as the fence we built—where what I own ends and where what you own begins.

Without boundaries, we give ourselves away. For example, before we had the fence built, Mean Mr. Mike and his barking Cujos had free access to our property in two ways. The first way was visually: they could see anything on our property without obstruction. The second way was physically, as his dogs would occasionally extend their leash to the limit, encroaching on our property. Previously, we were happy to give that to the tenants of the neighboring property. It simply wasn't a big deal.

As soon as we were mistreated, though, we were no longer interested in giving away what was rightfully ours.

In the absence of clearly defined boundaries, others will not know how much of our resources—our time, our emotion, our energy, our body—they are allowed to have access to.

The same is true in our relationships with others: in the absence of clearly defined boundaries, others will not know how much of our resources—our time, our emotion, our energy, our body—they are allowed to have access to. Most people will engage with respect and integrity when operating on this form of honor system. However, it only takes one uncaring or self-centered person to take as much of those resources as they can to leave the unprotected individual feeling taken advantage of or taken for granted. As we maintain control of the resources we own, though, we end up feeling more empowered, better about ourselves, and with a greater sense of being masters of our destiny.

About the Unskilled Fence Builder

The capacities to build bridges and fences are not mutually exclusive or opposed to one another. In fact, individuals who are skilled at initiating and sustaining healthy relationships have developed skills in both areas. Any given individual, though, probably will have a natural inclination or fluency in one area or the other. If you scored well on the bridge-building readiness assessment, then, the fence-building readiness assessment may eat your lunch. Alternatively, if you are not naturally a skilled bridge builder, you probably will excel with fence-building.

I have already noted that people who are not skilled at setting boundaries often end up feeling taken advantage of or taken for granted. Individuals who are not skilled at setting boundaries also have been described as being pushovers, and because they have little capacity for follow through, they end up losing the respect of the students, parents and colleagues with whom they interact. Examples of maintaining poor boundaries include acting on a first impulse to destructive ends, not being able to confront others to resolve conflict appropriately, not noticing when someone else displays a lack of boundaries, or ignoring when someone violates a boundary (particularly your own boundary).

Individuals who don't set boundaries often rationalize their behavior. Consider the following:

- A boundary is not necessary because they didn't mean to hurt me.

- A boundary is not necessary because what they damaged wasn't that valuable.

- A boundary is not necessary because I don't want to offend them or seem mean.

- A boundary is not necessary because they won't respect the boundary anyway.

Teachers who are too eager to feel accepted or be perceived as cool by students often fail in their attempts to establish appropriate boundaries. In worst-case scenarios, teachers who are unable to set appropriate boundaries with students are at risk of violating physical boundaries with students. The fact is that students actually hold higher respect for adults who can establish and maintain boundaries. The need to feel accepted or belonging can also limit a teacher's ability to set boundaries with colleagues or parents. Again, though, a healthy adult will hold higher respect for an individual who is able to set and maintain healthy boundaries.

I am reminded of a former teacher I met at a professional conference who was working at that time for an educational support agency. When I asked her why she left the classroom, she described a scenario that seemed void of boundaries.

"I put *everything* I had into it," she said. "I mean I really gave everything—my time, my money, my heart, and my mind. I totally went all out. After six years, I just gave out." I believe her difficulty lay in the fact that while her desire to make an impact was extremely honorable, her strategy to execute that desire was not sustainable.

What Is and Is Not Mine?

As you can see, setting poor boundaries makes for relationally muddy waters, and it truly is in the best interest of you and those around you to set and maintain healthy boundaries. How do you start? As you consider where you will establish your boundaries on the relational landscape of your calling, I encourage you to consider your stewardship of the following areas of your life: your time, your energy, and your expertise.

If you are employed, you have, in essence, entered into a contract to exchange your personal resources of time, energy, and expertise for the compensation of income, benefits, and a retirement package. Since you have made that commitment, then, it is reasonable for your employer to expect those things from you. How many hours per week must I give, though, and how many must I keep for myself? How much emotional energy must I give, though, and how much must I keep for myself? Did they purchase *all* of me?

Before we built the fence at our clinic, we had to have a surveyor come look at our land to establish what was legally ours and what was not. If only we could have a vocational surveyor consult with us to establish, based on our salary and job title, what we needed to give and what we did not in clear, exact, and measurable terms. Since we don't, the work–life balance tends to be evasive across all vocations.

I don't have a magic plug-in-the-variables formula for calculating where to draw boundaries in your vocation or mine, but I do often reflect back to the work of former U.S. president Dwight Eisenhower. "The urgent problems are seldom important ones," Eisenhower wisely observed. His approach to allocating his resources was based on a fundamental commitment to focusing on the important—not urgent—tasks. An illustration is often used of placing golf balls, marbles, sand and water in a jar. If we fill the jar first with water and sand, there will be no room left for the bigger marbles and golf balls. The idea is to fill the jars of our lives first with what is important, and then add to that the smaller things (many of which seem quite urgent in any given moment).

I've been discussing boundaries in a broad sense: big picture, how much should I allocate to my vocation? Let's focus the application to a more specific arena. Once I have found a big picture boundary with which I am comfortable, how do I set boundaries with individuals—my student who won't comply with my directives, my co-teacher who uses emotional manipulation to avoid her responsibilities, or the toxic parent who bullies me when her child does poorly in my class?

Again, we start by establishing what is mine and what is not. In the case of interpersonal relationships, what is mine includes my thoughts, my feelings, and my body. When my interaction with another violates my intellectual, emotional or physical freedom or safety, I am wise to establish a boundary. I establish a boundary by communicating clearly, firmly, and respectfully: "When you [name the behavior], it [name how it violates your boundary]. You do not have my permission to [repeat the behavior]." For example, "When you raise your voice at me, I feel insulted and condescended. You do not have my permission to speak to me that way. Please stop," or "I don't like it when you touch me there. You do not have my permission to touch me that way. Please stop."

One should never apologize for having boundaries, and you do not owe anyone an explanation for the boundaries you set.

There are a few key points to remember as you establish and maintain boundaries. First, one should never apologize for having boundaries, and you do not owe anyone an explanation for the boundaries you set. Also, if you know someone is likely to violate your boundary, be prepared to implement a consequence immediately; often, setting boundaries and implementing consequences triggers anger or other intense emotions in the boundary violator, so make sure you have the relational support you need so as not to be intimidated by their emotional response. Finally, remember that others have the right to set boundaries, too.

As you may have surmised, the effectiveness to which I am able to effectively set and maintain boundaries is linked closely to my sense of self. Do I perceive myself as valuable enough to have rights and to be protected?

Keep in mind as you establish your boundaries that some boundaries are permanent, but some need to be permeable. The level of physical contact between a student and a teacher? At some level, that is permeable. Under some circumstances, even a handshake may not be beneficial, but under another circumstance, a side hug might be completely appropriate. However, under no circumstances is sexual contact between a teacher and student ever appropriate. Similarly, there will be seasons throughout the school year in which I must bring work home to stay up-to-date. However, under no circumstances should my family life deteriorate because I've neglected relationships due to a long-standing habit of using my home time to work. We must continually evaluate and re-evaluate, then, which boundaries are appropriate and which need adjusting.

Table 5.1 Examples of Boundaries With Colleagues

Unhealthy Boundary With Colleague	Healthy Boundary With Colleague
"I'll call you Sunday morning again so we can finish that project we were working on." "Okay."	"I'll call you Sunday morning again so we can finish that project we were working on."
	"I understand that the project is important, but so is my family. I've reserved Sunday morning for them, so we'll need to find a different time."
"Did you hear about what that alcoholic Mr. Brand [a co-worker] did over the weekend?"	"Did you hear about what that alcoholic Mr. Brand [a co-worker] did over the weekend?"
"No, but it probably wouldn't surprise me. He's such a lush. What happened?"	"No. But what happens in his personal life probably isn't something we should be talking about here in the teachers' lounge. If it's really important, let's visit after work."

Table 5.2 Examples of Boundaries With Students

Unhealthy Boundary With Student	Healthy Boundary With Student
Students are allowed to take things off my desk and go through the drawers of my desk.	Students must ask me to give them things from my desk or to find things in the drawers of my desk.
If you break a rule, consequences will not be administered, or they will be administered inconsistently.	If you break a rule, consequences will be administered appropriately each time.

Table 5.3 Examples of Boundaries With Parents

Unhealthy Boundary With Parent	Healthy Boundary With Parent
"Yes, your son has been having trouble in my class. Just between you and me, the administration on this campus is completely incompetent, and you're not the only parent who has expressed concerns."	"Yes, your son has been having trouble in my class. To be honest, our entire faculty has been under enormous stress. But let's talk about how we can partner to help your son be successful."
"How I choose to run my class is none of your business. If you have a problem with me or my class, you can just take it up with the superintendent."	"I have tried to be very deliberate about how I established my class routine. Let's talk about what's not working for your child. If we can make adjustments, great. If not, maybe we can visit with the campus administrator to come up with a solution."

The Case of the Two Teachers

Remember Ms. Dunn? The one I crowned queen of directing emotion? Well, Ms. Robinson was the queen of protecting. I heard about the story from Mr. Wright, who was part of the meeting the day that Ms. Robinson earned the crown.

It turns out that Ms. Robinson and Mr. Wright had been called to a meeting in the conference room with Mr. Shields, the campus administrator. Mr. Shields, long ago, had confused decisive leadership with authoritarianism, and he had a long-standing reputation of bullying or manipulating employees to do what he wanted them to do. Over the course of his many years on his campus, Mr. Shields had fostered a culture of fear among the faculty and the students. Mr. Wright put it this way: "We have all just been walking around waiting for the next 'gotcha' moment. It was a beat down."

Ms. Robinson, Mr. Wright, and Mr. Shields entered the conference room and took their seats at the table.

"The reason we're here," Mr. Shields began, "is to discuss what you both have been doing to address the learning needs of your students in the content areas."

The meeting was fairly benign for the first fifteen minutes, as Mr. Wright described it. Ms. Robinson and he described to Mr. Shields their lesson plans and their collaborative efforts with their fellow grade-level teachers. It was going pretty well, he thought. And then, seemingly out of nowhere, Mr. Shields began to raise the volume of his voice.

"Look," Mr. Shields said emphatically, "I don't know what you two are thinking, but the bottom line is that I better get results out of you both." Then, he started to actually yell. "I'm just about done with you two! I'm pretty sure you have absolutely no idea what you're doing, and I wish that I had never asked you to be a part of this campus!"

I could sense the animation in Mr. Wright's voice as he recounted the story. His eyes were wide and he had an exasperated look on his face: "I mean, I knew the guy was a hothead, but I had never experienced anything like this. It was like he went from zero to ninety out of nowhere! He just starts going off on us. I kind of froze."

Fortunately, Ms. Robinson didn't freeze. Maybe it was because this was her first year on the campus, and she hadn't yet been trained to be intimidated by Mr. Shield's emotional manipulation. Very soon after Mr. Shields launched into his verbal tirade, Ms. Robinson held up both of her hands, palms faced toward him.

"Excuse me, sir, but you'll need to stop right there," she said, in a calm but firm tone. "I do not like being spoken to at that volume and in that tone. You do not have my permission to speak to me that way. Please stop."

"I was stunned," Mr. Wright told me. "I think Mr. Shields was too, because he just sat there and stared for a full ten seconds. I don't know that anyone had ever set that kind of boundary with him before."

Ms. Robinson's setting the boundary with Mr. Shields only escalated him further.

"*How dare you speak to me that way?*" Mr. Shields shouted. "I am the leader on this campus and you will do what I *tell* you to do!"

"And that's when it really got good," Mr. Wright told me.

Ms. Robinson calmly stood up from her chair, looked Mr. Shields in the eye, and said, "Mr. Shields, I just asked you not to speak to me in that volume or that tone of voice. Since you continue to do so, I am ending this meeting. Good day, gentlemen." And with that, Ms. Robinson left the conference room.

"And for the second time in less than a minute, Mr. Shields was speechless," Mr. Wright told me with a smile. "I mean, he just sat there and silently watched her walk out of the room. And then, after about fifteen seconds of silence, he immediately tried to save face."

"Okay," Mr. Shields barked at Mr. Wright, "now that I've dismissed her from this meeting, I still have you to deal with."

"So I realized in that moment," Mr. Wright told me, "that she had just stood up to this bully, and done so with incredible grace and professionalism. And you know what, I realized that I was done with the charade myself."

"Well," Mr. Shields demanded of Mr. Wright, "what do you have to say for yourself."

With that, Mr. Wright slowly stood up from his chair and walked to the door. "I have nothing to say, Mr. Shields. As Ms. Robinson just said, this meeting is ended."

After that meeting, Ms. Robinson and Mr. Wright requested a follow-up meeting with district level leadership to discuss Mr. Shields' behavior in that meeting, and their concerns about his leadership style. Mr. Shields was not removed from the campus, but over the course of the weeks that followed, he began to treat his staff with the dignity and respect they deserved.

What an amazing example of the power of effective boundary setting!

I know what some of you may be thinking. If you had done what Ms. Robinson did, you would have been fired. If you had requested a meeting with higher-level leadership, it never would have been entertained, and if it had been, nothing ever would have come of it. Those are the same possibilities that both Ms. Robinson and Mr. Wright faced. In the end, though, they realized the risks were worth it. They would rather be in the position of having to find a new job versus being in a position of having a job that they detested because of one highly toxic individual.

Protecting and Fence-Building: A Readiness Assessment

Now we know a bit more about how boundaries are essential to connecting. How naturally do protecting and bridge-building come to you? We created this assessment (see Table 5.4) to give us just a bit more of an empirical answer. Complete this assessment, and we'll tell you how your score compares with the sample group.

1 = Definitely Not True of Me

2 = Not Usually True of Me

3 = Undecided

4 = Usually True of Me

5 = Definitely True of Me

When you have completed the assessment, add your points. As with the bridge-building assessment, the highest you can score is a 150, which means you rated yourself a 5 on all 30 items. The lowest you can score is a 30, which means you rated yourself a 1 on all 30 items. The same sample of teachers that took the bridge-building assessment took this fence-building readiness assessment; we found an average score of 71. The lowest score was 60, and the highest was 113.

If you scored below 50, you probably are quite skilled at building fences and setting boundaries when compared to your colleagues. You probably understand the value of setting

Table 5.4 Protecting and Fence-Building: A Readiness Assessment

Thought/Feeling/Behavior	1 2 3 4 5

1. I have trouble making up my mind.
2. It's hard for me to say "no" to people, even when I know I shouldn't take on a responsibility.
3. It's hard for me to look another person in the eyes.
4. My classroom leadership style is characterized by threats and power struggles.
5. I find myself wanting to "rescue" people I sense are deeply troubled or very needy.
6. I tend to value the opinions of others over mine.
7. People use my things without asking.
8. Students take things from my desk without asking.
9. I've let people borrow things, and I'm afraid to ask for them back when things aren't returned and I need them.
10. I feel ashamed of things I've done in the past.
11. I feel ashamed of certain aspects of my current life.
12. I am uncomfortable feeling different from other people.
13. I'm afraid a parent will say bad things about me to my principal or other district leader.
14. I'm afraid students will reject me if I give them consequences for their inappropriate behavior.
15. I tend to feel anxious or afraid something bad will happen.
16. I will help others, even if it means I will suffer or do without something important.
17. My happiness depends on feeling accepted by my colleagues.
18. My happiness depends on feeling accepted by my students.
19. My happiness depends on feeling validated by my students' parents.
20. It's often hard for me to know what I really want in life.
21. It's often hard for me to know what I feel about any given issue.

Thought/Feeling/Behavior	1 2 3 4 5
22. I feel an emptiness inside.	
23. I hate spending time alone.	
24. I tend to take on the mood of people around me.	
25. I tend to take on the ideas and opinions of people around me.	
26. I have a difficult time receiving constructive feedback.	
27. I have a history of romantic relationships with individuals who have been hurtful to me.	
28. Usually, when someone hurts me, I won't say anything about it.	
29. I tend to ignore too much inappropriate student behavior in my classroom.	
30. I usually end up doing more than my fair share of work in a group project.	

limits and expecting your authority over yourself and over your classroom to be respected.

If you scored between 61 and 81, your fence-building skills probably are very comparable to your colleagues. Your capacity to establish boundaries is neither a strength nor a weakness.

If you scored above 91, you probably are not a natural fence builder when compared to your colleagues. You probably tend to hesitate to set effective boundaries for fear of the relational loss that may accompany the boundary.

Key Point Summary

♦ Boundaries are about defining what belongs to me and what does not.

♦ Without boundaries, burnout is imminent.

♦ The difference between the urgent and important.

"Integrate: to make whole by bringing all parts together."
Merriam-Webster's Dictionary

6

Towards Integration

In Chapter 1, we told you that a primary philosophical under-pinning in our approach to relationships is a focus on the internal. To restate and reiterate that idea, we believe that after you have implemented external, structural interventions to develop relational success (things like campus-wide positive behavior supports and effective classroom management procedures), you will then need to venture into the internal work we have outlined here to truly maximize your capacity to develop life sustaining and life changing relationships with your students, their parents, and your colleagues. In many ways, apart from formal and manualized academic and behavioral interventions, our "self" is the most important and potentially most effective intervention on a campus.

As I conclude, I will review the four practices, and offer you questions to consider as you ponder your state of well-being in each area:

Practice #1: Reflecting on Calling

If I am not experiencing deep, rich, and rewarding relation-ships with my colleagues, my students, and their parents, I will consider the following questions to develop my skill of REFLECTING:

1. Have I sifted through life-shaping events in my life, both positive and negative, to establish a sense of meaning about my purpose in life? Have I identified my calling? Have I established a personal mission statement documenting why I am choosing to show up to my campus each day?

2. If I have, am I living a life of emotional, physical, spiritual, financial, and occupational balance? If I am not living a life of balance and am experiencing a deep void in any certain area of my life, am I seeking to fill that void through my vocation? In other words, am I seeking satisfaction in my calling, or am I finding satisfaction in the totality of my life and taking satisfaction to my calling.

Practice #2: Directing My Emotion

If I am not experiencing deep, rich, and rewarding relationships with my colleagues, my students, and their parents, I will consider the following questions to develop my skills of DIRECTING:

1. Has someone who expressed an emotion inappropriately physically or emotionally wounded me?

2. Have I forgiven them?

3. As a result of a single experience or ongoing exposure to a hurtful situation, have I closed myself off from experiencing any emotion?

4. Apart from experiencing (i.e., simply acknowledging) an emotion, am I insecure about expressing any particular emotion?

5. Have I expressed an emotion inappropriately that has been physically or emotionally harmful to a colleague? A student? A parent? Myself? If so,

have I asked that person to forgive me (including self-forgiveness)?

6. If I realize that I cannot experience and/or express any given emotion, what steps do I need to take to increase my capacity in that area?

Practice #3: Connecting by Building Bridges Across Difference

If I am not experiencing deep, rich, and rewarding relationships with my colleagues, my students, and their parents, I will consider the following questions to develop my skills of CONNECTING:

1. Did I grow up in a family where relational connection was not emphasized, encouraged or practiced?

2. Have I habitually valued task completion over relationships?

3. If I have been hurt by someone who is different from me, have I forgiven that person and everyone who is like them and different from me (e.g., all other people of the same sex, race, ethnicity, religious belief system, generation, etc.)?

4. How much do I practice pushing through the discomfort of difference to really get to know people who don't look like me, sound like me, value what I value or believe what I believe?

Practice #4: Protecting by Building Fences

If I am not experiencing deep, rich, and rewarding relationships with my colleagues, my students, or their parents, I will consider the following questions to develop my skills of PROTECTING:

1. Did I grow up in a family where relational connection was not emphasized, encouraged or practiced?

2. Am I afraid to set boundaries with others for fear of
   being rejected or otherwise losing a sense of security
   about relational proximity?

I've been quite fortunate to have gone back and thanked many
educators who have made a difference in my life. I've often
thought it would be amazing, though, to be able to sit with all
of them in a room, put on my psychologist hat, and really interview them to glean from them all the insight I possibly could.
There are so many questions I'd ask. Honestly, based on what I
know about each of them, I think their answers would be pretty
simple and straightforward. I honestly don't think they would
talk about academic or behavioral interventions that revolu-
tionized their approach in the classroom and on the campus. I
think each of them would simply say something to the following effect:

> *If I'm honest, there were days, a few seasons even, when
> being an educator felt like little more than a job. But under-
> neath it all, I knew I was placed on this earth to impact my
> students; I carried a deep and abiding passion to "grow"
> young men and women. Of course, I experienced intense
> and uncomfortable emotions across the course of my lifetime
> in education—anger, frustration, confusion, sadness—but
> I always took the high road. I always remembered my
> position of influence, and I always sought to maintain the
> integrity of my platform. I learned to reach out and connect
> when necessary, and I learned to step back and set a bound-
> ary when necessary. I ran the race, and by God's grace, I
> finished well.*

In the Words of Polonius ...

I (Adam) don't know where or who I would be today had educators not built relationships with me and constructed a platform in my heart upon which they spoke truth into my life
about my identity. I don't know that I ever would have gone to
college. I do know that once I did go to college, the fact that I
majored in English was a direct result of the influence of three

of my high school English teachers, women who taught me, apart from the deep life-lessons about my identity, the value of the spoken and written word. Although my college years were difficult in many ways, the hours I spent between the covers of my Riverside Shakespeare anthology are among my sweetest memories. In honor of Mrs. Brewer, Mrs. McRoberts, and Mrs. Exley, I leave you with a quote from *Hamlet*. Although Polonius is often viewed as being a chief counselor sorely lacking in good judgment, his parting advice to his son, Laertes, in Act 1 captures a truth relevant to us and worth repeating:

> This above all: to thine own self be true,
> And it must follow, as the night the day,
> Thou canst not then be false to any man.
> Farewell, my blessing season this in thee!
> *Hamlet*, Act 1, Scene 3, 78–82

Bibliography

Asher, D. (2007). *Who gets promoted, who doesn't, and why: 10 things you'd better do if you want to get ahead.* Berkeley, CA: Ten Speed Press.

Bahman, S., & Maffini, H. (2008). *Developing children's emotional intelligence.* New York, NY: Continuum International Publishing Group.

Bailey, B. A. (2001). *Conscious discipline: 7 basic skills for brain smart classroom management* (revised ed.). Oviedo, FL: Loving Guidance, Inc.

Bloomquist, M. L. (1996). *Skills training for children with behavior disorders: A parent and therapist guidebook.* New York, NY: The Guilford Press.

Bloomquist, M. L., & Schnell, S. V. (2002). *Helping children with aggression and conduct problems: Best practices for intervention.* New York, NY: The Guilford Press.

Bottke, A. (2011). *Setting boundaries with difficult people: Six steps to sanity for challenging relationships.* Eugene, OR: Harvest House Publishers.

Boynton, M., & Boynton, C. (2005). *The educator's guide to preventing and solving discipline problems.* Alexandria, VA: Association for Supervision and Curriculum Development.

Breaux, A., & Whitaker, T. (2006). *Seven simple secrets: What the best teachers know and do.* Larchmont, NY: Eye on Education, Inc.

Breaux, A., & Whitaker, T. (2010). *50 ways to improve student behavior: Simple solutions to complex challenges.* Larchmont, NY: Eye on Education, Inc.

Breaux, A., & Whitaker, T. (2012). *Making good teaching great: Everyday strategies for teaching with impact.* Larchmont, NY: Eye on Education, Inc.

Breaux, A. L., & Wong, H. K. (2003). *New teacher induction: How to train, support, and retain new teachers.* Mountain View, CA: Harry K. Wong Publications, Inc.

Burgess, D. (2012). *Teach like a pirate: Increase student engagement, boost your creativity, and transform your life as an educator.* San Diego, CA: Dave Burgess Consulting, Inc.

Burke, J. (2008). *Classroom management: How to establish positive discipline, organize your classroom, and manage your teaching time.* New York, NY: Scholastic Inc.

Canter, L., & Canter, M. (1993). *Succeeding with difficult students: New strategies for reaching your most challenging students.* Bloomington, IN: Solution Tree Press.

Charney, R. S. (1991). *Teaching children to care: Management in the responsive classroom.* Greenfield, MA: Northeast Foundation for Children.

Clark, R. (2003). *The essential 55: An award-winning educator's rules for discovering the successful student in every child.* New York, NY: Hyperion.

Cloud, H., & Townsend, J. (1992). *Boundaries: When to say yes, how to say no, to take control of your life.* Grand Rapids, MI: Zondervan Publishing House.

Cloud, H., & Townsend, J. (1998). *Boundaries with kids: When to say yes, when to say no, to help your children gain control of their lives.* Grand Rapids, MI: Zondervan Publishing House.

Colverd, S., & Hodgkin, B. (2011). *Developing emotional intelligence in the primary school.* New York, NY: Routledge.

Crowe, C. (2009). *Solving thorny behavior problems: How teachers and students can work together.* Turners Falls, MA: Northeast Foundation for Children, Inc.

Cummings, C. (2000). *Winning strategies for classroom management.* Alexandria, VA: Association for Supervision and Curriculum Development.

Cummings, E. E. (2002). *The enormous room.* New York, NY: Dover Publications, Inc.

Curwin, R. L., Mendler, A. N., & Mendler, B. D. (2008). *Discipline with dignity: New challenges, new solutions.* Alexandria,

VA: Association for Supervision and Curriculum Development.

Delpit, L. (1995). *Other people's children: Cultural conflict in the classroom*. New York, NY: The New Press.

Fenstermacher, G. D., & Soltis, J. F. (1998). *Approaches to teaching* (3rd ed.). New York, NY: Teachers College Press.

Fiore, D. J. (2001). *Creating connections for better schools: How leaders enhance school culture*. Larchmont, NY: Eye on Education, Inc.

Fiore, D. J., & Whitaker, T. (2005). *Six types of teachers: Recruiting, retaining, and mentoring the best*. Larchmont, NY: Eye on Education, Inc.

Gartrell, D. (2004). *The power of guidance: Teaching social-emotional skills in early childhood classrooms*. Clifton Park, NY: Delmar Learning.

Goldstein, D. B., & Kroeger, O. (2013). *Creative you: Using your personality type to thrive*. Hillsboro, OR: Beyond Words Publishing, Inc.

Goleman, D. (1995). *Emotional intelligence: Why it can matter more than IQ*. New York, NY: Bantam Dell.

Greenberger, D., & Padesky, C. A. (1995). *Mind over mood: Change how you feel by changing the way you think*. New York, NY: The Guilford Press.

Hagerty, B. B. (2009). *Fingerprints of God: The search for the science of spirituality*. New York, NY: Penguin Group.

Hansen, D. T. (1995). *The call to teach*. New York, NY: Teachers College Press.

Hargreaves, A., & Fullan, M. (2012). *Professional capital: Transforming teaching in every school*. New York, NY: Teachers College Press.

Harris, S. (2005). *Bravo, teacher! Building relationships with actions that value others*. Larchmont, NY: Eye on Education, Inc.

Hartney, E. (2008). *Stress management for teachers*. New York, NY: Continuum International Publishing Group.

Harvard Business Review. (2010). *HBR's 10 must reads on managing yourself*. Boston, MA: Harvard Business Review Press.

Jalongo, M. R. (2008). *Learning to listen, listening to learn.* Washington, DC: National Association for the Education of Young Children.

Kessler, R. (2000). *The soul of education: Helping students find connection, compassion, and character at school.* Alexandria, VA: Association for Supervision and Curriculum Development.

Klaus, P. (2007). *The hard truth about soft skills: Workplace lessons smart people wish they'd learned sooner.* New York, NY: HarperCollins Publishers.

Krovetz, M. L. (2008). *Fostering resilience: Expecting all students to use their minds and hearts well* (2nd ed.). Thousand Oaks, CA: Corwin Press.

Landsman, J., & Lewis, C. W. (2006). *White teachers/diverse classrooms: A guide to building inclusive schools, promoting high expectations, and eliminating racism.* Sterling, VA: Stylus Publishing, LLC.

Marshall, M. (2005). *Discipline without stress, punishments, or rewards.* Los Alamitos, CA: Piper Press.

Marzano, R. J. (2007). *The art and science of teaching: A comprehensive framework for effective instruction.* Alexandria, VA: Association for Supervision and Curriculum Development.

Marzano, R. J., Marzano, J. S., & Pickering, D. J. (2003). *Classroom management that works: Research-based strategies for every teacher.* Alexandria, VA: Association for Supervision and Curriculum Development.

McKay, M., Fanning, P., Lev, A., & Skeen, M. (2013). *The interpersonal problems workbook: ACT to end painful relationship patterns.* Oakland, CA: New Harbinger Publications, Inc.

McKay, M., Wood, J. C., & Brantley, J. (2007). *The Dialectical Behavior Therapy skills workbook: Practical DBT exercises for learning mindfulness, interpersonal effectiveness, emotion regulation & distress tolerance.* Oakland, CA: New Harbinger Publications, Inc.

Muhammad, A. (2009). *Transforming school culture: How to overcome staff division.* Bloomington, IN: Solution Tree Press.

Nagel, G. (1994). *The Tao of teaching: The special meaning of the Tao Te Ching as related to the art and pleasures of teaching.* New York, NY: Donald I. Fine, Inc.

Nieto, S. (2003). *What keeps teachers going?* New York, NY: Teachers College Press.

Orange, C. (2008). *25 biggest mistakes teachers make and how to avoid them* (2nd ed.). Thousand Oaks, CA: Corwin Press.

Palmer, P. J. (1993). *To know as we are known: Education as a spiritual journey.* New York, NY: HarperCollins Publishers.

Palmer, P. J. (1998). *The courage to teach: Exploring the inner landscape of a teacher's life.* San Francisco, CA: Jossey-Bass Inc.

Riggenbach, J. (2013). *The CBT toolbox: A workbook for clients and clinicians.* Eau Claire, WI: Premier Publishing and Media.

Riley, P. (2011). *Attachment theory and the teacher-student relationship: A practical guide for teachers, teacher educators and school leaders.* New York, NY: Routledge.

Rouse, P. E. (2007). *Every relationship matters: Using the power of relationships to transform your business, your firm, and yourself.* Chicago, IL: American Bar Association Publishing.

Ryan, K., & Cooper, J. M. (1975). *Those who can, teach* (2nd ed.). Boston, MA: Houghton Mifflin Company.

Whitaker, T. (2010). *Leading school change: Nine strategies to bring everybody on board.* Larchmont, NY: Eye on Education, Inc.

Whitaker, T. (2013). *Dealing with difficult teachers* (2nd ed.). New York, NY: Routledge.

Woititz, J. G. (1993). *The intimacy struggle: Revised and expanded for all adults.* Deerfield Beach, FL: Health Communications, Inc.